THE TWO JERUSALEMS

IN PROPHECY

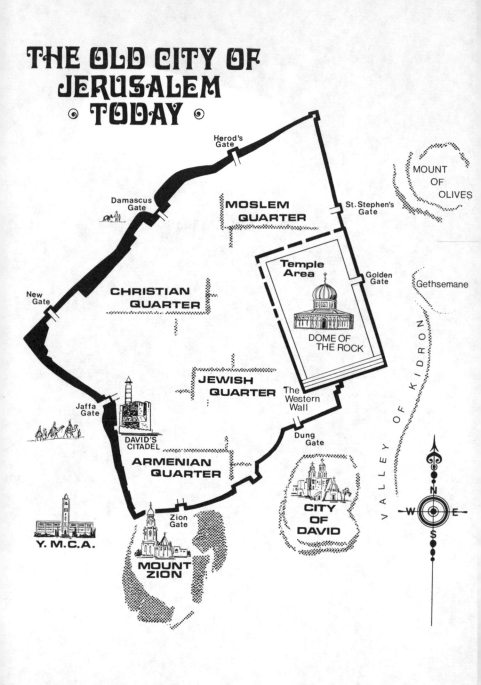

The Two Jerusalems in Prophecy

by

DAVID CLIFFORD

An Artist's Impressions by

F. NEWMAN TIMMIS

LOIZEAUX BROTHERS
Neptune, New Jersey

FIRST EDITION, NOVEMBER 1978

Library of Congress Cataloging in Publication Data

Clifford, David (Leonard), 1911-
    The two Jerusalems in prophecy.

    Bibliography: p.191
    1. Bible—Prophecies—Jerusalem. I. Title.
BS649.J38C58   220.1'5   78-14922
ISBN 0-87213-081-9

Printed in the United States of America

Dedicated to
WINIFRED EVELYN
My Devoted Partner
in the
Highest Service
for
Almost Forty Years.

Bible quotes are from the

New American Standard Bible

unless otherwise stated

CONTENTS

AN ARTIST'S IMPRESSIONS

FOREWORD

With the publication of this book on Biblical prophecy Dr. David Clifford is seen to reveal the more recent trend of his ministry. Through the years his main work has been in Christian education and in this field there is no one I admire more. It was while he was engrossed in the training of young men and women for the service of Christ around the world, that I first became acquainted and associated with him. He was at that time (1961) the principal (and founder) of the Moorlands Bible College in the south of England, which I considered to be the finest Bible college in Britain. I was pleased to serve in that school as a member of the visiting faculty. Now, therefore, I am happy to commend this work to the general reader and to evangelical Christians in particular, for careful reading and study.

In *The Two Jerusalems in Prophecy* Dr. Clifford shows the importance both cities must play in a right understanding of the prophetic Scriptures: Old Jerusalem in Palestine and New Jerusalem above. His expositions of the Scriptures reveal that the one Jerusalem will be the earthly throne of the Heavenly King, while the other will become the heavenly home of earthly people redeemed by the blood of the Lamb. The tragedies and triumphs of old Jerusalem and the glories and grandeur of the New Jerusalem are set out fully from the Word of

God and with the inspiration characteristic of the writer's ministry.

This book will be read with real profit by all those who "look for His appearing."

JOHN WESLEY WHITE

Toronto, Canada

INTRODUCTION

Prophecy and Jerusalem are inseparable. Who can write a thesis on prophecy without dwelling much of the time on the city of Jerusalem? Most of eschatology is centered around this remarkable city which, without doubt, must become the focal point on earth for the fulfillment of the program God has revealed for this ailing planet.

The reason for this marriage between Jerusalem and prophecy is seen in the fact that this is the City of God. His anointed King secured it, His Presence was known in it, His people of old were the inhabitants of it, His Son was sent to it. In spite of Christ's rejection His hand has been upon it and will be so again. The realization of the prophetic plan for God's ancient people will be focused on this city of earth.

Similarly, prophecy and the New Jerusalem are inevitably linked. God has promised a full salvation for those who are "in Christ," ending in glory, and the preaching of the evangel must surely include the preaching of the hope, which is the glorious climax of this "so great salvation." "Because of the hope laid up for you in heaven, of which you previously heard in the word of truth, the gospel, which has come to you" (Colossians 1:5-6).

The end of our salvation therefore is in Heaven, from whence also we look for the Saviour, and all prophecy is centered in Him. He is the Desire of Israel and the Hope

11

of the Christian; He is the Deliverer so sorely needed by the nations and the Redeemer of this groaning creation; He is the Son of God once rejected and He is God's King who is to reign when the hour for His vindication has arrived. He will reign over the earth with the Church from the New Jerusalem in the heavens. In the prophetic Word, the Church is seen to have a heavenly calling. This for the Christian spells out the words: "The New Jerusalem."

Although both Jerusalems are linked with predictions for the future, it is still true to say that the one great purpose of Scripture prophecy is to show that God will both vindicate and glorify His Son; yet both His vindication and His glorification will be in these two cities which bear the name *Jerusalem*. In the place of His rejection He is to be glorified and receive the honors of earth, and in the midst of His own in the New Jerusalem, in Heaven, He is to be worshiped and adored and that for all eternity.

Some students of the Word will attempt to show that the purpose of God to vindicate His Son is not the only design of prophecy and they will mention the fact that God intends to keep His promises and covenants to His people of old. They will say that one purpose is to show that God will declare to all mankind His immutable Sovereignty, or to manifest openly to principalities and powers His glory and grace in the Church, and the infinite wisdom of His transactions with men, but by and large all these other suggestions fall into their places under the general purpose here stated that above all other intentions it is God's will to vindicate the Son of His love, and glorify His name before all His creation.

A clarification of the comparisons and the contrasts between these two Jerusalem cities, their inhabitants, their positioning, and the timing of their appearances and functioning is the purpose of this book. These last-day prophecies must concern every Christian, because of the perilous times in which we are now living, and one may well imagine that many of those who read these lines will soon be taking part (if they are not already) in the fulfillment of scriptural predictions concerning the end of the age. Even though no one knows the day nor the hour when the Lord will come, or the times and "epochs which the Father has fixed by His own authority," events are beginning to move rapidly toward a climax, on the international and Middle East scenes, and with regard to Jerusalem itself.

The hope and callings of both Israel and the Church of Jesus Christ are seen epitomized in these two cities of Jerusalem and their future roles in prophecy. There are similarities, but there are important distinctions, too, which certainly should be made in the right interpretation of prophecy.

The old was the city of David; the new is the city of David's greater Son.

The old is earthly, the new is heavenly.

The old rejected her King at His first coming, the new will crown Him King of all, following His second coming.

The old has been under Gentile domination for nearly 2,000 years, the new will always be under Christ's control.

The old became the city of warfare, the new is the true city of peace.

The old will be the capital of the earthly kingdom, the new will be the bride of Christ.

The old is the type, the new is the antitype.

There will always be Jerusalem, the old city will arise yet again even following the further troubles which may come to her as the Scriptures reveal. It is the eternal city in the true sense of the word. The long and fluctuating history of this amazing ancient city has many lessons to teach the world, and history, as we know, has a way of repeating itself from time to time. For our purpose, however, the historical review must be quite sketchy, because in the main our object is to show the old city of Jerusalem and the new heavenly city of Jerusalem in their respective roles in the future. Nevertheless, there are three ways in which Old Jerusalem speaks to the world: historically, spiritually, and prophetically.

Historically, through its checkered vicissitudes, Jerusalem is a confirmation through the years of the scriptural Word: "Righteousness exalts a nation, But sin is a disgrace to any people" (Proverbs 14:34).

Spiritually, through its rebirth and unification, Jerusalem is a reminder that failure is not final with God. Not that God always gives peoples and nations another chance, but God will certainly fulfill all that He has promised. "If we are faithless, He remains faithful; for He cannot deny Himself" (2 Timothy 2:13).

To Abraham and to David God made these unconditional promises, and He is always true to His Word, "for the gifts and the calling of God are irrevocable" (Romans 11:29).

Prophetically, too, Jerusalem speaks to the world, through its prospects and hopes according to the divine pattern laid down in the prophetic Scriptures. When she repents of her sin and godlessness, and in particular of her rejection of her Messiah (according to Zechariah 12 she will do so), then she will be free and her deliverance will be real and lasting. Her King will reign in righteousness and Jerusalem will be the joy of all the earth in a far greater and fuller sense than ever it has been in the past, or can be at present.

One more thing should be said. Nowhere in Scripture is the law of double reference, and the idea of first partial and then final fulfillment of prophecy, seen more than in the unfolding of eschatology in relation to the Old and New Jerusalems. The first or partial fulfillment is included in the realm of realized eschatology, but a great deal of what we shall see still not fulfilled as yet, but which must surely come to pass, is to be counted as an essential part of unrealized eschatology. In these momentous days mere interest will develop into excitement and blessed anticipation for the well-informed and diligent student of God's Word.

> Jerusalem in Palestine, the golden chosen place,
> The city of God's rightful King, of Israel's earthly race;
> How soon 'twill be when we will see
> Jerusalem from Gentiles free?
>
> Jerusalem above on high, a part of Heaven come down,
> The dwelling of the saints of God, of Him who wears the
>   crown;
> From thence they'll reign with heav'nly train,
> When earth is filled with praise again.

1

JERUSALEM, THE HOLY CITY

It seems incongruous, these days in which we live, to call even one of this world's cities "holy." Most of our cities now seem to be centers of unholy practices, with muggings and shootings and many other acts of violence and crime. But Jerusalem is named the holy city of the world mainly because of the three great religions which have their roots firmly established there: Christianity, Judaism, and Islam. Christianity commenced in it, Judaism claims it because King David captured it, and Islam reveres it because of its famous Mosque of Omar, situated within its walls and on the temple site. Hence the Arabs refer to Jerusalem as "El Kuds," that is, "Holy Town."

"If I Forget Thee, O Jerusalem"

After King David captured the fortress of Zion from the Jebusites in 1000 B.C., he chose it and extended it to be his capital and stronghold. God chose it also, that is the extended Zion, now called Jerusalem, and He caused His Presence to be known within her shrine.

"Great is the LORD and greatly to be praised,
In the city of our God, His holy mountain,
Beautiful in elevation, the joy of the whole earth,
Is Mount Zion in the far north,
The city of the great King" (Psalm 48:1-2).

17

It seems that the enemy has been busy through the centuries seeking to destroy it, for his objective has always been to thwart the divine program and God's purposes in the earth. However, the Jews themselves brought much evil upon their city by their infidelity to God, as is described in detail by both major and minor prophets in the Old Testament, and their eventual rejection of Jerusalem's rightful King, God's unique Son. "He came to His own, and those who were His own did not receive Him" (John 1:11). They plainly said, "We do not want this man to reign over us" (Luke 19:14). The Gentiles have for many years overrun the city, but in 1967, after so long a time, the Jews once more liberated it. Of course they had never forgotten their beloved city and never could do so. That which David said in the Psalms is always remembered: "If I forget you, O Jerusalem, may my right hand forget her skill. May my tongue cleave to the roof of my mouth, if I do not remember you, If I do not exalt Jerusalem above my chief joy" (Psalm 137:5-6).

Still in unbelief in their true Messiah, the Jews through Zionism are now attempting to make Jerusalem once more "the joy of all the earth" and Israel's eternal city, but having refused the One who came in His Father's name, one day, sooner than we think, the Jews will receive "one who will come in his own name," so said their true Messiah. They will again be deceived as the prophetical Scriptures declare, until the abomination of desolation, as spoken of both by Daniel the prophet and the Lord Jesus, will be set up in the new temple which is to be built in or near the city. Their opposition to this blasphemous act will mean that once more Jerusalem will be overrun and trodden down by the Gentiles.

This, however, will be only for a few years, but it will be the time of great tribulation and judgment, spoken of in detail in the book of Revelation. At the conclusion of it God will send His son, their Messiah, finally and completely to liberate them and their city. Then, and not till then, will the times of the Gentiles be fulfilled, and Jerusalem will become the city of God's King.

Another Jerusalem Will Appear

At this precise time, however, a new, a heavenly Jerusalem, will begin to play an important role in the affairs of men generally, but it will especially concern those who are found trusting Jesus Christ, the Son of God, as their own Saviour and Lord. This New Jerusalem will be their city, in fact they themselves will form it, and this heavenly Jerusalem will be their eternal home, for theirs is a heavenly calling. It will be this new city, however, which will be the center of Christ's authority over the earth during His millennial reign. Then it will be that the psalmist's prophecy will be fulfilled, when he by the Spirit said, "and men shall be blessed in Him" (Psalm 72:17), that is: all those in the New Jerusalem reigning with Him over the earth and all those on the earth sharing in the peace and prosperity and righteousness of His glorious reign will be blessed indeed.

That there are *two* Jerusalems playing important roles in the future is without question if our views are based upon the Scriptures of truth. The writer of the Epistle to the Hebrews mentions both Jerusalems when he says, "Ye are come to Mount Zion *and* to the heavenly Jerusalem" (Hebrews 12:22). Mount Zion of course is that part of Jerusalem built on Zion's hill, and the heavenly Jerusalem is this New Jerusalem, the home of the redeemed. Later on in the Epistle he says, "Let us therefore go forth unto Him outside the camp . . . because here we have no continuing city but we seek one to come" (Hebrews 13:13-14). Two cities are also seen here: first, Jerusalem of old, which is not a continuing city for those who have left Judaism for Christ and who have gone outside that city with Him, bearing His reproach; and secondly, the city to come, which Christians seek as their permanent abode. Again, the Apostle Paul in Galatians 4:25 said, "Agar . . . answereth to Jerusalem which now is, and is in bondage with her children"; but in the next verse he states, "But Jerusalem which is above is free, [and] . . . the mother of us all"; this means, of course, the mother of all those whose faith is in Christ Jesus.

As Jerusalem became the scene of much of our Lord's life and ministry and passion, it has thereby become the home or center of the Christian faith and, to many millions of people, the religious capital of the world.

On the east side of the city is Mount Moriah, which originally was the site of the threshing floor of Ornan the Jebusite, and this is the place which became known as the hill of Zion or David's city. When David first captured it from the Jebusites it was but a small fortress, named "Jebus" in the book of Joshua. Jerusalem later became known as Salem, which is an abbreviation, and also is named "Zion" on numerous occasions in the Scriptures. This part of the city which is built on Mount Zion is 2,581 feet above sea level, and one can imagine the winding mountainous approach by road from such a place as Jericho only thirteen miles away, but which is some 900 feet below sea level. "Jerusalem" means "the habitation of peace," but is often called, in the Scriptures, the city of God, for it is the capital of the only kingdom on earth established up to this time by God Himself, and God chose to put His name there.

Then also note what David had to say in Psalm 110: "The LORD said unto My Lord, Sit Thou at My right hand, until I make Thine enemies Thy footstool." He, with the seer's eye, was looking forward to the millennial age, when Christ will reign from the New Jerusalem over the nations of the earth. But in the next verse he adds, "The LORD will stretch forth Thy strong scepter from Zion, saying, Rule in the midst of Thine enemies. Thy people will volunteer freely in the day of Thy power" (Psalm 110:2-3).

Our Lord is seen here in both of the cities of Jerusalem: at God's right hand in the heavenly Jerusalem and in Zion. It is true to say that He will reign over the earth from the New Jerusalem and on the earth from the old city in Palestine.

Beautiful for Situation

The city of Jerusalem is situated between the Mediterranean Sea and the Jordan River. There are mountains all around the city, forming a strong triangular defense. She has no river, no sea, and no ancient trade routes. However, Jerusalem was the city that God Himself made the center on earth for the worship of His Name and the place from which His laws were proclaimed. It was from this city that the majority of His prophets uttered their warnings and gave divine calls to His people and to all of earth's inhabitants.

Jerusalem's Temples

Through the years, three great temples of magnificence and splendor have been built within the walls of Jerusalem: Solomon's temple in 960 B.C.; that of Zerubbabel in 515 B.C.; and Herod's temple, which took forty-six years to construct and was still being built in the time of our Lord, only being completed a few years before the siege of Jerusalem by Vespasian. This resulted in the destruction of this third temple by Titus of Rome. The west wall of the last temple remains until this day and is commonly known as "the wailing wall." It is the place to which the Jews have resorted for very many years (except when barred from it during the years of the divided city, 1948-1967) to remember their exiled brethren scattered around the world and to pray to God for the restoration and rebuilding of the city and its temple. That another temple, in or near Jerusalem, is to be built in the future is evident in Scripture from the words of the Prophets Ezekiel, Zechariah, and Malachi, and especially because of what the Saviour Himself said about the time in the future when the Jews will actually see the abomination of desolation set up in the temple in Jerusalem. This has never yet happened, and indeed it was still future, even in our Lord's day.

A new temple is also called for if there is to be a right understanding of the prophecies concerning the earthly calling of the Jews and how that is contrasted with the future of the Church and its heavenly calling.

The West Wall of Herod's Temple
The Wailing Wall

In the following paragraph these contrasts are set out clearly, but the details are left to be dealt with in later chapters.

Contrasts Between Old and New Jerusalem
Between God's Earthly People and the Church

God's earthly people were promised the kingdom on earth centered on Old Jerusalem. The Church was promised a place in Heaven, centered on New Jerusalem.

God's earthly people will flock to Old Jerusalem at the end of the age. The Church will be caught up to New Jerusalem at the end of the age.

God's earthly people face the tribulation and yet another besieging of Old Jerusalem. The Church faces the glory and the blessing of New Jerusalem.

God's earthly people will inhabit Old Jerusalem and Palestine. The Church will inhabit and form the New Jerusalem in the heavens.

God's earthly people will be saved by Christ at the deliverance of Old Jerusalem. The Church will be the bride of Christ, secure in New Jerusalem.

God's earthly people will rule with Christ from Old Jerusalem. The Church will share the reign of Christ from the New Jerusalem.

God's earthly people will worship their Messiah and King in Old Jerusalem. The Church will worship her Lord and King in New Jerusalem.

God's earthly people and the city of Old Jerusalem will be a praise among the nations. The Church and the New Jerusalem will be the light and the blessing of the nations.

2

JERUSALEM'S CHECKERED HISTORY

Jerusalem is first mentioned in the Bible in Genesis 14:18. This is the record concerning Melchizedec, king of Salem, priest of the most High God, who met Abram after his victory at the battle of the kings. There Melchizedec brought bread and wine for a feast to celebrate Abram's triumph that day, and there he blessed Abram. The date of this occasion was approximately 1900 B.C.

The next mention of the city in the Scriptures is in Joshua 700 years later, when Zion was the capital of Adoni-zedek. Joshua, in the allocation of the land of Canaan, gave this area to Benjamin, who was not able to drive out the Jebusites. This is understandable in the light of its fortified mountainous situation. But many years later King David took this almost impregnable stronghold. He succeeded where others had failed, by invading the fort through the tunnel which led underneath and inside the walls of the city from the spring Gihon outside.

It is true that a statement at the commencement of the book of Judges suggests that Jerusalem was captured by the children of Judah at an early period in the settlement of Israel in the land of Canaan. However, F.F. Bruce in his book, *Answers to Questions*, gives Pearce Hubbard's explanation that the Jerusalem of Judges 1:8 and of Joshua 10:1,5,23, and 12:10 was a settlement of the southwestern hill, distinct from the well-fortified Jebusite settlement on the southeastern hill, which remained in Canaanite hands until David's day. Jebusite Jerusalem was apparently confined to the hill of Orphel, which was the stronghold of Zion.

When David was reigning as king in Hebron, he undoubtedly saw the wisdom of capturing Zion's hill. As it is recorded, he took it by divine decree. Hence, this conquest over the Jebusites was the commencement of God's own plan for the city. It was first called "David's city" by David himself soon after he captured it; and so he made Zion, or "Jerusalem" as it was soon to be called, his capital, and he built his own palace there and extended the city east and north and fortified it even more.

The Ark of the Covenant Brought to Zion

It was to Zion's hill that David brought the ark of the covenant of the God of Israel to the tent which he had erected for it. He had been concerned about his neglect of the ark at the commencement of his reign, but the determination to find it and bring it to his city grew stronger and stronger:

> "I will not give sleep to my eyes . . .
> Until I find a place for the LORD. . . .
>
> Behold, we heard of it [the ark] in Ephratah;
> We found it in the field of the wood. . . .
> Arise, O LORD, to Thy resting place;
> Thou and the ark of Thy strength" (Psalm 132:4-8).

David Brings the Ark of the Covenant
Home to Zion

The ark was a small wooden box lined with gold, four feet by two-and-a-half feet by two-and-a-half feet. The top or lid of the ark was of solid gold; this was called the "mercy seat," and God had said, "There I will meet with you" (Exodus 25:22). Fixed to the ark, but over it, were two cherubim images facing antithetically and looking downward. Inside the ark were the tables of stone, the Law, as given to Moses, also the manna, and Aaron's rod which had budded. The ark itself and everything to do with it are all very significant in a spiritual way, but most of all the ark always denoted the Divine Presence, and is by Christians now seen to be a beautiful picture or type of our Lord Jesus Christ.

Unfortunately for Israel, the ark of the covenant had been captured earlier by the Philistines, but eventually they had released it and it remained in Kirjath-jearim for some time. David decided, however, that he must bring it home to Zion and place it in the Tabernacle which he had erected for that purpose on the hill of Zion. IIe appointed Asaph and his brethren to minister before the ark, and it was Asaph who wrote Psalm 78 to show that the planned transference of the sanctuary, including the ark, from Shiloh in the north to Mount Zion, was by divine appointment: "He chose the tribe of Judah, the Mount Zion, which He loved, And He built His sanctuary" (Psalm 78:67-69).

Jerusalem was fortified still further by King Solomon, son of David, who also built within the city the first temple of extensive proportions and brilliant architecture: "Then Solomon began to build the house of the LORD in Jerusalem on Mount Moriah, where the LORD had appeared to his father David . . . on the threshing floor of Ornan the Jebusite" (2 Chronicles 3:1).

And again we read: "Solomon finished the house of the LORD and the king's palace, and successfully completed all that he had planned on doing in the house of the LORD" (2 Chronicles 7:11).

Jerusalem Destroyed

Following the death of Solomon in 930 B.C. there came the revolt of the ten tribes with their separation to the north, with the city of Samaria as their capital. The two tribes still remained in the south of the country and had Jerusalem as their capital. This latter city was known thereafter as the "capital of Judah." Much later on, when our Lord met the woman of Samaria at Sychar's well, the Samaritan woman thought she should remind our Lord of the distinction they both must have known only too well. She said to Him: "How is it that You, being a Jew, ask me for a drink since I am a Samaritan woman?" (For Jews have no dealings with Samaritans.) . . . Our fathers worshipped in this mountain [Gerizim]; and you people say that in Jerusalem is the place where men ought to worship" (John 4:9,20).

Jesus then explained in the simplest terms that the place to worship was not so important after all, but it was the spirit of the worshiper which must be right in any approach to God. "Worship the Father in spirit and truth," He said (John 4:23).

It was, therefore, following the dividing of Israel between north and south that the checkered history of the city of Jerusalem really commenced. It was besieged seventeen times in all and twice razed to the ground. First of all, it was plundered and pillaged by Shishak, king of Egypt; later by Joash from the northern tribes (although this time Jehoiachin surrendered the city to save it from a long and weary siege). Again it was overrun by Nebuchadnezzar from Babylon, following a siege for one-and-a-half years which had resulted in acute famine. He actually burned the city, and the Temple and the palace were likewise destroyed. According to the report which Nehemiah later received, Nebuchadnezzar had even broken down the walls completely and left them as heaps of rubble. This happened in the year 586 B.C.

Before the Temple was destroyed, however, it was completely ransacked, and the holy vessels and valuable furniture of the sanctuary were removed and eventually taken to Babylon. The princes of the city and the men of substance were also taken away, together with the artisans who were skilled in all manner of work. In all, there were ten thousand transported to Babylon, and only the poorest of the people of Jerusalem were left behind in the city.

The Reason for the Babylonian Captivity

The captivity of Judah in Babylon was to last seventy years, and this the Prophet Daniel discovered one day as he sat reading while in Babylon, for he himself was one of the captives. He was poring over the then recent prophecy of Jeremiah, one of his contemporaries, who by the Spirit of God had said: "For thus says the LORD, 'When seventy years have been completed for Babylon, I will visit you and fulfill My good word to you, to bring you back to this place' " (Jeremiah 29:10).

The purpose of this stated period of captivity is given in the plainest terms in Scripture. Note first how the law itself was given by God for the good of the land and the people: "The seventh year you shall let it rest and lie fallow, so that the needy of your people may eat. . . . You are to do the same with your vineyard and your olive grove" (Exodus 23:11).

Later on a warning, also in love, was given by God to His people about the land He was to give them: "You, however, I will scatter among the nations . . . as your land becomes desolate. . . . Then the land will enjoy its sabbaths all the days of the desolation, while you are in your enemies' land. . . . It will observe the rest which it did not observe on your sabbaths, while you were living on it. . . . For the land shall be abandoned by them, and shall make up for its sabbaths while it is made desolate without them. They, meanwhile, shall be making amends for their iniquity, because they rejected My ordinances. . . . Yet in spite of this . . . I will not reject them" (Leviticus 26:33-35,43,44).

In the historical recording of the captivity in Second Chronicles the reason is given by divine inspiration why the catastrophe of the captivity overtook His people: "But they continually mocked the messengers of God, despised His words. . . . Therefore He brought up against them the king of the Chaldeans . . . to fulfill the word of the LORD by the mouth of Jeremiah, until the land had enjoyed its sabbaths. All the days of its desolation it kept sabbath until seventy years were complete" (2 Chronicles 36:16-17,21).

God is righteous in all His ways and works and God's timing is always right. Therefore seventy years in captivity was the length of time ordained by God Himself to make reconciliation between His people and Himself for their disobedience concerning the law He gave

them about the land they were to farm, and into which
He had brought them. The context also explains how the
Lord stirred up the spirit of Cyrus, king of Persia, at the
conclusion of these seventy years to make a proclamation
throughout all his kingdom: "He [God] has appointed
me to build Him a house in Jerusalem, which is in Judah.
Whoever there is among you of all His people, may his
God be with him! Let him go up to Jerusalem which
is in Judah" (Ezra 1:2-3).

Jerusalem Restored

It was in 538 B.C., therefore, that Zerubbabel
returned to Jerusalem with 42,360 men to commence rebuilding the Temple. Their resources were so few, and opposition grew so strong, that they were forced to dis-
continue the building. Then Nehemiah arrived a few years
later, and his main burden was to rebuild the walls of the
city. This work was completed and the walls dedicated
with great ceremony and praise to God. Nehemiah en-
closed the actual city of Jerusalem, as well as Zion, within
these new walls. Artaxerxes gave a commission to Ezra the
priest some years later who, together with a large party of
priests and Levites and Nethinims (1,777 in all), returned
to recommence the building of the Temple. Ezra was
careful to take time to pray and publicly confess his
nation's sins, and this was followed by certain reforms
being made and put into operation at once.

The Temple Desecrated

All Palestine, including the city of Jerusalem,
fell to the Seleucidae invaders in the year 198 B.C., but

it was during the reign of the Syrian king, Antiochus the Fourth (Epiphanes), when the land and the city were recovering somewhat from this attack, that dangerous intrigue in relation to the priesthood was being fostered in Jerusalem. This came to the notice of Antiochus and enraged him, and eventually brought him to the city in 170 B.C. to deal once and for all with this misbehavior. He made a resolve to utterly exterminate the Jews and their religion. He made a decree that there must be heathen worship, and he himself, quite brazenly, entered the holy of holies to do mischief. The altar was piled up with profane things, and pig's flesh was offered to the god Zeus on an altar set up on top of the altar to Jehovah. Many Jews heroically attempted to resist, but alas in vain, and Antiochus carried off to the north the golden altar, the candlestick, and the table of shewbread from the Temple, together with its vessels and utensils. The city was again burned with fire, and the walls once more broken down. But was Jerusalem finished?

Jerusalem Defended by Maccabees

Five years afterwards, a noble Jew named Judas Maccabeus, one of five sons of Mattathias, who led a short rebellion, gathered together six hundred faithful Jews and defended Jerusalem against an army of sixty thousand men led by Lysias. This is the prayer he prayed before the battle was joined that day:

Blessed art Thou, O Saviour of Israel,
Who didst quell the violence of the mighty man
By the hand of Thy servant David

> And gavest the host of strangers into the hand of
> Jonathan the son of Saul and his armorbearer,
> Shut up this army in the hand of Thy people Israel,
> And let all those that know Thy name
> Praise Thee with thanksgiving.

Maccabeus himself died as he fought the enemy, and his people mourned him with these words, "How is the valiant man fallen, that delivered Israel!"

His courageous brothers continued the struggle against tremendous odds for some years following. Jerusalem, however, was again besieged by the Romans and captured in B.C. 63. Twelve thousand Jews fell in the battle.

Antipater, the first procurator in Judea, had a son named Herod who was proclaimed king of Judea in 40 B.C. Three years later the Maccabean house lost its last ruler in a blood bath as Herod and his mercenaries streamed into the city. After a short time of rigid rule, however, Herod's policy was to favor the Jews somewhat, giving them some freedom to worship their God. In fact, a restoration of the Temple began in B.C. 20 by the order of this king. This was to be called thereafter "Herod's Temple." There was continuing discontent, however, with resultant uprisings, until in A.D. 7 Judas of Galilee led a powerful insurrection, only to be subdued with ruthless firmness by the Romans. The priests of Jerusalem, including Caiaphas, who was the high priest for eighteen years, attempted to live peaceably for some time with the occupying power. Pilate was procurator of Judea during the last part of Caiaphas' period of power.

The population of Jerusalem steadily increased during these decades until at the time of our Lord there were twenty-five thousand people living in the city. During the festivals, this number is said to have expanded to sixty thousand, and later on at the time of the Roman siege, with a great influx of pilgrims and Jews from areas outside seeking protection, it was estimated that 600,000 were in Jerusalem. So Jerusalem became a city of sieges for fifteen centuries. There were plunders and surrenders, revolutions and famines, restorations and rebuildings, burnings and bondage until this same place became the city of Christ's rejection.

Jerusalem, the City of Confusion

Isaiah in his prophecy refers to Jerusalem as the city of confusion, and although it was at first named "the city of God" (and God is not the God of confusion, as the Apostle Paul declares), Jerusalem had been put to confusion because of the infidelity of its people to God. Although often warned by the prophets who came to the city to call them to repentance, the people heeded them not, but even worse, they heeded not Christ Himself. When Christ came to His own, His own did not receive Him. They rejected God's Son, His Well Beloved, their true Messiah and King.

3

JERUSALEM IN THE TIME OF OUR LORD

Jesus was first brought into the city, which was to become the place of His crucifixion, when He was but a few days old. He was presented to the Lord by Mary and Joseph, who made an offering at the same time of a pair of turtle doves or two young pigeons. It was in the Temple that Simeon recognized Jesus, by the Spirit's guidance, as God's salvation for men, and it was at the same time that Anna the prophetess pointed to Jesus as the Redeemer of Israel. The next time that Jesus came to this unsettled city was when he was a boy of twelve years. He found His way into the Temple again. He also realized that He must soon be about His Father's business and said so. "Your father and I have been anxiously looking for You," Mary said, but His significant reply was, "I had to be about My Father's affairs" (Luke 2:48-49), referring to Jehovah God, who is the Father of the Son Incarnate. But they did not understand.

Following His outstanding ministry of teaching and healing in the region of Galilee, Jesus went up to Jerusalem again; that was in the fall of A.D. 29 at the time of the feast of tabernacles. The feast had already commenced when He arrived. He began at once preaching to the crowds surrounding the Temple, but the rulers of the Jews were by this time planning how they might take Him. These rulers in Jerusalem formed the Sanhedrin, which was the council of the Jewish religion. It was composed mostly of men from the sect of the Sadducees, but the Pharisees were represented also, not so strongly, although they were noted for their teaching of the Old Testament law.

At the feast of dedication some weeks later Jesus again put in an appearance, but left the city quite soon when He knew that some were intent on His arrest there and then. But He also knew that His time had not yet come. The news quickly spread around Jerusalem in A.D. 30 that Jesus had raised Lazarus from the dead in the village of Bethany, only a short distance away. There was much curiosity among the people and many flocked after Him, hoping to see further signs. There was much concern developing among the Sanhedrin members because of His amazing popularity, and they sought a way to arrest Him again, but they feared the people who were beginning to see Him as a prophet of God.

After being away from the city preaching the gospel of the kingdom, teaching His disciples, and healing the sick, He turned to His own and said: "Behold, we are going up to Jerusalem, and all things which are written through the prophets about the Son of Man will be accomplished. For He will be delivered up to the Gentiles . . . they will kill Him; and the third day He will rise again" (Luke 18:31).

For the Lord Jesus alone, death was to be an obedience, as Paul stated to the Philippians. (For all other men death is a necessity!)

Triumphant Entry into Jerusalem

Some pilgrims, on their way to the city from the north, met Jesus and His disciples en route to Jerusalem, it seemed, and on the last section of the journey, over the Mount of Olives and into the city, they formed the crowd which showed great pleasure and some excitement when Jesus rode towards the city on an ass. But He Himself was seen weeping over the city, even amidst the rejoicing of the people. For them this was difficult to understand until He spoke, and revealed what was in His heart about the city. They thought He was riding to a throne, but He knew that He was riding to a cross. They thought He was about to judge His enemies; but He knew that His enemies were about to crucify Him. They thought this was the start of a great following; He knew that this was the start of a great forsaking. They thought this was His hour of glory; He knew that this was His hour of agony.

Jesus Weeps Over the City

Three times it is recorded that Jesus wept. Once over a family's sorrows in Martha's home; once more over His own sorrows in the garden of Gethsemane—yet not His own, for "Surely our griefs He Himself bore, and our sorrows He carried" (Isaiah 53:4); and again here on the Mount of Olives He wept over a nation's sorrows. He could see the judgment of Jerusalem and the nation of the Jews coming quickly upon them. He spoke about the Temple and the city being brought to desolation, all because "they knew not the day of their visitation" (Luke 19:44). God's salvation had been visiting them in the Person of Jesus Christ and they knew it not. "You shall see me no more," He added, "until you say, 'Blessed is He that cometh in the name of the Lord' " (Luke 13:35). When He entered the city, Jerusalem was wild with excitement. Jesus went into the Temple, first to drive out from its court the merchants, reminding all and sundry that this was God's house of prayer, and then He healed crippled people and others who needed His touch. The chief priests saw the wonderful things He did and heard the boys of Jerusalem shouting, "Hosannah to the Son of David," and they asked Him by what authority He did these things, but He wisely declined to answer. He did say, however, that the stone which the builders refused had become the head of the corner. They knew that He was referring to their rejection of Him, but they could do nothing towards arresting Him, for all the people took Him to be a prophet.

Jesus' Temple Prophecy

As He left the Temple His disciples showed Him the temple buildings, in their splendid setting, but He once again spoke sadly of their coming destruction. "Not one stone shall be left upon another, all will be thrown down," He said, and they asked Him when that would be. His reply was to encourage them to look for such signs as nations rising up in war against one another, famines spreading around the world, an abundance of earthquakes, and finally when the abomination of desolation, as spoken of by Daniel the prophet, was set up in the holy place, those in Judea should flee to the mountains for protection. "This generation," He said, speaking of the generation which sees the beginning of these sorrows and signs, "will not pass away until all these things take place" (Matthew 24:34). Events therefore will move very quickly at the end, He was saying. The Son of Man will come in His glory, and the King will say to those placed on His right at the judgment of the nations, "Come, you who are blessed of My Father, inherit the kingdom."

Later on in that week our Lord held the Passover feast with His disciples in the upper room of a house in Jerusalem tenanted by one of His friends, the "good man." This man gave the Lord his biggest and best room and placed all his furniture at the Lord's disposal. It was from this hour of communion with His disciples in this upper room that the Lord Jesus went out into the garden of Gethsemane, where His soul was exceedingly troubled, and where He prayed, "Thy will be done." He arose at once and gave Himself into the hands of the mob which sought His life, and He was led back into Jerusalem. First He was brought before the ex-high priest Annas for preliminary questioning, and then He was taken to Caiaphas, who was high priest that year. In Caiaphas' palace the Sanhedrin was sitting; probably they had gathered for this special purpose, the judging of Jesus. In answer to the question, "Are You the Christ, the Son of God?" He openly endorsed His previous claims and said, "You have said it . . . hereafter you shall see the Son of Man sitting at the right hand of Power and coming on the clouds of heaven" (Matthew 26:63-64).

Jesus was now brought to Pilate, the governor. Perhaps there was an agreement beforehand that He should be brought? The answer that Pilate received from Christ, together with the message he received from his wife about having nothing to do with this just Person, made Pilate ill at ease. As he sought to let Him go, he confessed, "I find no guilt in this man" (Luke 23:14). However, this verdict was not accepted by the priests and the people, who said He ought to die, adding, "His blood be on us and on our children" (Matthew 27:25). The priests, therefore, being moved with envy stirred up the people, who cried, "Let Him be crucified" (Matthew 27:23).

Outside the City Wall

Through the gates of the city of Jerusalem they led Him to Calvary and to His crucifixion. The disciples were now dispersed; the city of Jersualem was now disturbed; the land of Palestine was now darkened and dreadful; but the world was soon to be turned upside down, because "God raised Him up again."

All Jerusalem knew that the tomb in which they had put the body of Jesus was empty a few days later. The chief priests knew this fact only too well, for they had started the rumor throughout the city that His disciples had stolen the body of Jesus. The evidences of this tremendous fact still hold good today after over 1900 years. Not only was He seen by Mary, but by all the apostles, as Peter said; not only was Thomas convinced, but over five hundred brethren saw Him at one time. Not only were the brothers (after the flesh) of our Lord changed into believers at the resurrection of Christ, but Saul of Tarsus was changed into the beloved Apostle Paul through his meeting with the risen Saviour. Not only was the abject fear of the disciples turned into boldness, but they turned the world upside down, all because He had shown Himself to them after He had risen from the dead.

"What gave rise to the resurrection faith if it was not . . . the resurrection fact?" wrote F.F. Bruce in *The Dawn of Christianity.*

It was the ancient city of Jerusalem, therefore, which witnessed the most dastardly act of history, the crucifying of Christ, the Son of God's love, turned into the glorious triumph of all times: His resurrection by the power of God on the third day. Thus He was declared to be, by His miracles and ministry, by His dying and His living again and appearance to His chosen witnesses on eight different occasions, the promised Messiah and the Son of God.

Calvary
Outside the City Wall

4

JERUSALEM AND HER NEW
FIRST CENTURY FELLOWSHIP

Six or seven weeks after the stupendous events, seen in our last chapter, had come to pass in Jerusalem, something else took place, another happening just as momentous if not so spectacular, which changed the course of history. On this occasion a new time period commenced in God's prophetic plan, for it was then that the Church age came into being with the coming of the Holy Spirit. The Church, according to Paul, is "a dwelling of God in the Spirit" (Ephesians 2:22), so there was no Church until the descent of the Holy Spirit. This is what took place in the city of Jerusalem at the feast of the first fruits of the wheat harvest, known as the feast of Pentecost. There were three main festivals in the year for the Jews, the feasts of unleavened bread, of tabernacles, and of Pentecost. To take part in all these, pilgrims journeyed to Jerusalem from all areas of Palestine and many other Mediterranean lands.

On this occasion, the disciples of Jesus were together in one building in the city, and there was perfect unity and a spirit of expectancy among them. Suddenly an unusual sound was heard and a striking spectacle filled their gaze, for the promised Spirit of God had descended from Heaven and He was seen resting on each one of them in the form of, or similar to, tongues of flame.

This gracious Holy Spirit was the promise of the Father and the Son, indeed He was called the Spirit of Promise. The Saviour had said He would send Him from the Father to them, not only to be with them but to be in them. Although He was everywhere all the time as the omnipresent Spirit of God, He then came in a new way to be resident both in the hearts of His own and in the Church He formed that day. Believers in Christ at that time were first baptized by the Spirit into the body of Christ, and indeed filled with the Holy Spirit at the same time, there in the city of Jerusalem. This was a direct fulfillment of the words of our Lord, who promised, "You shall be baptized with the Holy Spirit not many days from now" (Acts 1:5).

The Spirit immediately controlled them and caused them to speak aloud in languages they did not know, but which were proved to be languages of the Jews from all over their known world. Naturally these visitors were amazed beyond telling, for they not only understood the languages which the speakers themselves did not, but they heard the wonderful works of God proclaimed with no uncertain authority.

The mocking, as well as the fear which ensued, brought the Apostle Peter into action in the forefront of the group, and his Pentecostal sermon is recorded in the second chapter of the Acts of the Apostles. It was not only powerful, but prophetic. The central theme was the Saviour, His death, His resurrection, and His present authority, and the call was to repentance and to faith in Christ.

Jerusalem saw the beginning of a great movement of the Spirit, which spread around the world and has lasted until this day. Three thousand on that first day believed the Word. They confessed their faith in Christ in baptism and were added to the number of the disciples and to their fellowship. It was in the very city where our Lord was crucified that God was now commencing to vindicate His Son, the rejected King. The process will continue until His authority is recognized throughout the world, and His glory fills the whole earth.

When our Lord said to His own, "You shall be witnesses unto Me beginning at Jerusalem," He not only wanted them to commence where they were at the time (not at home, for some of them lived up in Galilee), but His desire was surely that they should offer salvation in His name in the very city where He was rejected and crucified, and that it should be offered first to the Jews of Jerusalem.

In this early fellowship of the disciples of Jesus, Mary His mother was in Jerusalem with them, accompanied by two of her younger sons (by Joseph), James and Jude. There is no record of His brothers believing in Jesus as the Messiah previous to this, in fact the record says, "for not even His brothers were believing in Him" (John 7:5), that is, during His three years' ministry. But after the resurrection, being convinced themselves that He was alive and was all He had claimed to be, both James and Jude became open followers of their brother after the flesh. James especially was counted a leader of the church at Jerusalem following Pentecost, and he, together with Peter and John, were known as "pillars of the church" (as Paul described them after his meeting with the disciples and apostles in the city).

Jesus of Nazareth, or Jesus the Nazarene, left His stamp upon the city of Jerusalem with no uncertainty, for His ardent followers became known as the Nazarene party. It might have appeared to some that this group was simply one of the many which were associated with Judaism, but although there were Jews at Pentecost, and the Christian Church commenced with Jews, the Holy Spirit was not limited (and never is) and soon Samaritan believers shared the same gift of the Spirit. Christianity, therefore, was not simply a development of Judaism, but a new faith, and an exclusive way to God and to His salvation, since the death and resurrection of His Son.

This group and their teaching became quite attractive to the people of Jerusalem and many thousands believed at different times, among them a number of priests. Among their opponents, however, were the Sadducees, but these were not very successful in trying to curb the activities and effective ministry of the apostles and believers. (It was later on and outside of the Jerusalem area, that the disciples of Christ were called Christians.)

The gifts of the Spirit were manifested in the city, and wherever the apostles preached and journeyed God saw fit in His sovereignty to demonstrate the veracity of their message concerning His Son, by giving signs through the operation of the gifts (for God does not use all the gifts all the time, but only in His divine will and times). "In the name of Jesus" was the phrase often used by the apostles and this was honored by God in showing signs and wonders and miracles and healings. There was great power, great unity, and great grace upon them all.

Persecution in the City

The apostles were imprisoned in Jerusalem now and again, and by God's intervention set free. They were warned by the chief priests not to speak in the name of

Jesus, but they decided to obey God rather than men, even the men of the Sanhedrin. At one time, this council brought an accusation against Stephen, through whose ministry and miracles the irresistible power of God was evident. He was charged with blasphemy and eventually rushed out of the city and stoned to death. Jerusalem therefore witnessed the first martyrdom of the Christian Church, and so did Saul of Tarsus. He was a renowned student, under the teaching of Gamaliel, a doctor of the law. Saul was a willing witness, for he had been taught to oppose the Nazarene sect, and this he did most vigorously. He became the leader in a wave of persecution which swept the Jerusalem church, to the extent that many believers left the city for other parts of Judea and Palestine. Saul felt it his duty to seek them out and bring them back to the city for trial. However God had other plans for them, and indeed for Saul himself.

On one of these errands of persecution against the Christians he was thrown to the ground by a dazzling light from Heaven, and spoken to directly by the risen Christ, who said, "Saul, Saul, why are you persecuting Me? . . . I am Jesus whom you are persecuting" (Acts 9:4-5). Saul was converted at once; He owned Jesus as Lord, and cried, "What shall I do, Lord?" (Acts 22:10) Ananias, a servant of the Lord, was sent to help Saul to recover from this experience, for it had left him blind. Not only were his eyes opened, but he obediently submitted to believer's baptism, and before Ananias left, he made sure that Saul was also enjoying the experience of being filled with the Holy Spirit, given over completely to the Spirit's control.

Soon afterward he was named Paul and became an apostle, God's chosen vessel to bear His name among the

Gentiles, and to bring the gospel to Europe. There was nothing lacking in courage or in conviction as Paul preached. On one occasion while in Jerusalem, Paul accepted Christian hospitality from Peter and no doubt he was glad to get some firsthand information concerning the life and ministry of the Lord Jesus and about the commencement of the Church. The Lord in a vision warned Paul and told him to leave Jerusalem quickly, and when he did so he soon realized that God was sending him further afield among the Gentiles.

A young man named John was cousin to Barnabas, a companion of Paul, and was later given the Roman name Marcus. One day John Mark left the city with these two to go to Antioch, and later he was invited to go on one of their missionary journeys. However, the young man failed before the half-way stage, and returned home to Jerusalem. No doubt he too loved Jerusalem, or was it the fellowship of the new Christian church there which he missed so much? Whatever the reason, he gave up the missionary work. The Lord however did not give him up, for with God failure is not final, and Paul not only received him again later, but testified that he was profitable to him in the service of Christ.

Another convert to the faith, a man equipped by the Spirit with the gift of evangelist, was Philip. He soon left Jerusalem to evangelize in distant parts. While he was in Samaria a spiritual revival broke out and multitudes turned to the Lord. At this time there was an interesting visitor in Jerusalem from Ethiopia, no one less than the treasurer to the queen mother of Nubia. He was evidently a proselyte to the Jewish faith and came to worship God. Philip was prompted by the Lord to leave his fruitful ministry in Samaria and find this Ethiopian on his way home from Jerusalem. At Gaza they met and the evangelist told him about Jesus from the prophecy of Isaiah 53. He believed, was baptized, and went on rejoicing.

First Christian Council

The all-important council of Jerusalem was held in A.D. 49. Most of the believers held the view that circumcision was still essential, but others from Antioch and Asia Minor and in the churches founded by Paul, believed that faith in Christ alone was sufficient for fellowship with God and His people. Judaistic preachers who went out from Jerusalem sought to bring Christians into the bondage of the old law, once more, and there was a plea from all sides for immediate action and discussion. Paul and Barnabas, with others, came from Antioch and met the Jerusalem leaders of the Church, and the doctrine of liberty in Christ won the day. There was to be no other consideration apart from faith in Christ necessary for either salvation or fellowship with fellow believers who were Jewish. (See F.F. Bruce's *The Dawn of Christianity*.)

A return visit to Jerusalem had been uppermost in Paul's mind when he was in Macedonia. He was anxious to be there at Pentecost, so his calls at Troas and Miletus, Tyre, and other ports en route were very brief. At Caesarea he and Luke, the beloved physician, received hospitality from Philip the evangelist, for he had moved there from Jerusalem. At this time Agabus came to Caesarea from Judea to give a prophecy that Paul would be bound by the Jews when he reached Jerusalem, and would be handed over to the Gentiles. Nevertheless Paul continued the journey with the words, "I am ready, not to be bound only, but also to die at Jerusalem for the name of the Lord Jesus." He was received joyfully by

James and the elders, but it was not long before Jerusalem was in uproar again when Paul was seen in the Temple. He was beaten and carried into the castle, the fortress of Antonia. After some hours he was allowed to give a speech in his own defense, before the crowds outside. The audience became divided among themselves when he spoke concerning the resurrection of the dead, and Paul was almost lynched. He was rescued just in time by the soldiers and carried into the castle. That night the Lord appeared to him in a vision, both to comfort and counsel him: "Take courage; for as you have solemnly witnessed to My cause [in] Jerusalem, so you must witness at Rome also" (Acts 23:11). At the first opportunity Paul asked for a passage to Rome, when he said, "I appeal to Caesar," and they said, "to Caesar [Rome] you shall go" (Acts 25:11-12). However, he was forced to wait for two years, first in Jerusalem and then in Caesarea, before he finally set sail for Rome.

The ship became violently storm-tossed, and hope of being saved was gradually abandoned. However assurance was given to Paul by God Himself, who said, "Do not be afraid, Paul; you must stand before Caesar" (Acts 27:24). It was confirmed that the ship would go down, but none of the persons on board would be lost, so the apostle encouraged the crew: "Keep up your courage, men, for I believe God, that it will turn out exactly as I have been told" (Acts 27:25). Some reached land on broken pieces of the ship or on boards, but they were all saved and Paul eventually reached Rome, only to be put in prison in that city, yet in the center of the will of God. It was from Rome he wrote the four prison letters under the inspiration and control of the Spirit of God, and thus the first century church of Jerusalem expanded and increased its influence from that city to others and around the world.

5

JERUSALEM IN A.D. 70 AND THROUGH THE YEARS

The Church in Jerusalem was again beginning to suffer intense persecution in A.D. 61. About the time that the procurator Festus died, a council of judges was formed to try the Apostle James. The result of this trial was that James was stoned and bludgeoned to death, because he refused to disassociate himself with the ever-increasing Nazarene group, as the new Christian Church was called.

The moderate party in Jerusalem received help from the Jewish king, Agrippa the Second, who ruled in the north. But it was to no avail, because the extremists fought on relentlessly and took control of the city by the fall of 66, the Roman garrison having been eliminated by this time. Anti-Jewish massacres occurred soon afterwards until Cestius Gallus of Syria proceeded south to conquer Jerusalem. The defenders strongly fortified the temple area, and thus thwarted the attack, although it was a bitter struggle and Gallus finally retreated in disorder.

This victory meant that the extremists began to think that even Rome was not able to stand against them, but it was a vain hope. Vespasian eventually intervened with his might. First he overcame the opposing forces throughout Galilee by the year 67, but nearly twelve months later, although he intended to proceed to take Jerusalem, having heard of the death of Nero, he himself was called back to Rome and there he was made emperor. Vespasian then gave Titus command of the forces in

Palestine, and an order to overcome all resistance, especially that of Jerusalem.

Although within one year practically all of Judea had yielded to Titus, Jerusalem still stubbornly resisted his Roman army. In 70, however, the city was besieged with the utmost determination. Nevertheless, the Jewish defenders refused the terms offered to call off the siege. Slowly but surely the Romans advanced until most of the city was destroyed, with the exception of part of the west wall of Herod's temple. Those who remained in the city were captured and slain; many hundreds were crucified, some upside down, and the streets are said to have flowed with blood. This is the siege and the desolation envisaged by Christ when He wept over the city from the mount of Olives, and was also the fulfillment of the crowd's declaration when they cried, "His blood be on us and on our children." This coming of the Romans to destroy the Jews and their city was not, however, the fulfillment of Christ's promise to come again, as some have said, for this must certainly be seen as God sending His judgment upon them. At this time they did not repent and turn to their true Messiah, and it was Christ Himself who had warned them: "Behold, your house is being left to you desolate, and I say to you, you shall not see Me until the times come when you say 'Blessed is He who comes in the name of the Lord' " (Matthew 23:38-39). That cry of repentance and hope is still awaiting a future fulfillment.

The Great Dispersion from Judea

The complete destruction of Judea was ordered by Rome in 135. This meant that the people who had survived and were still living in the area at once decided to disperse abroad, and they were soon found at the ends of the earth. This dispersal has remained virtually complete until the present time, with the exception of the return to Israel of some two-and-a-half million Jews, through the efforts of Zionism, during the last century. The effect of the desolation of Judea and the dispersion of the Jews left the country dead (to all intents and purposes) for many centuries. This was so in spite of the fact that Hadrian rebuilt Jerusalem soon after the dispersion.

The city came under Byzantine rule for three hundred years after its partial restoration, although during that time the Persians held it for fifteen years. In 638 Omar ben Hatav put Jerusalem in the hands of the Moslems, and fifty years later the famous Mosque of Omar was built on the temple site, over the summit of Mount Moriah, by Abd-al-Malik. This is now called the Dome of the Rock. Towards the end of the eleventh century the Seljuk Turks invaded the city. The cruelty they meted out led directly to the Crusades, and Jerusalem came into Crusader hands in 1099. Their control lasted nearly ninety years, and the city became prosperous once more.

The taking of Jerusalem from the Crusaders by Saladin in 1187 saw the reestablishment of a Jewish settlement in the city. However, it was destroyed yet again by the Mongols in 1259. The Turks then captured the city once more through the sultan Selim early in the sixteenth century. The walls were rebuilt by him and his successor Suleiman in 1542, and these remain to this day. These Ottoman Turks occupied and controlled the city of Jerusalem until World War I, when General Allenby conquered Palestine and entered Jerusalem on foot without a shot being fired, on December 9, 1917.

Jerusalem Under the British

The occupation of Palestine by the British forces from 1918 to 1920 was the turning point in the history of Israel (although the Jews were often frustrated in many ways), and this was followed by a mandate over the country, assigned to the British by the League of Nations, which lasted until 1948. It was the Balfour declaration, made by the British foreign secretary, A.J. Balfour, in 1917, which commenced the move towards a new nation of Israel; it said, "His Majesty's Government views with favor the establishment in Palestine of a national home for the Jewish people." It is true that the British were slow in making progress to this end, as their policy was also to remain friendly with the Arabs. By the beginning of World War II, there were still less than half-a-million Jews in Palestine, as a restriction on Jewish immigration was severe, and a strict control over the sale of land to the Jews was enforced. The wholesale slaughter by the Nazis of some six million Jews during the years of World War II created noticeable and worldwide sympathy for them, to the extent that there was far more interest in giving the Jews a national homeland at the conclusion of hostilities. This widespread feeling brought no pleasure to the Arabs, however, and by 1947, with various proposals for Palestine gaining ground and a partition plan by the United Nations on the internationalization of Jerusalem being made, bitter conflict arose between Arabs and Jews.

On May 14, 1948 the National Council of Tel-Aviv proclaimed the new State of Israel, and the next day the mandate was relinquished by the British. War immediately followed and the Arabs laid siege to the old city, which was captured by Jordan and held for eighteen years. Nothing would satisfy the Jews, however, but Jerusalem; so in July of the same year (1948) Jewish Jerusalem was proclaimed Israeli territory. This meant that the Israeli government, the Knesset, was free to move to the city and Jersualem was proclaimed the capital of Israel. The Arab nations refused to acknowledge Israel for many years, and the Arab refugee problem became an open sore.

A boundary line and a narrow no-man's-land was established between Israel and the Hashemite kingdom of Jordan. This ran so close to Jerusalem that the old walled city was just inside Jordan, and the western newer part, was in Israel. The hill Zion, however, was part of this suburb on the south side of the southwestern corner of the city wall, and the development of this section was rapid indeed.

So for more than nineteen hundred years since the rejection of Christ and His crucifixion outside the city wall, Jerusalem has had a sad and bitter story to tell about her capture and recapture, her defense and desolation, her plunder and poverty, her building and rebuilding. Her people have been slaughtered or scattered, conquered or crucified, and the marvel is that the Jews are found today back in their own city and in their own land, a virile although small nation, with great prospects, although not without grievous fears. The reason for their survival and partial restoration must be the overruling hand of the Almighty. God has a great future for the Jews, and He has promised them a much larger area of land for their final homeland. God will use them after He has refined them in the reign of His Son over the earth. They will look on Him whom they have pierced, and will mourn and repent for their past rejection of Him, and all Israel shall be saved.

6

JERUSALEM TODAY

The city of Jerusalem in Palestine is said to be the geographical center of the earth. That she is truly the heart of the Holy Land is without question, for people from all parts of the world love her and every stone within her gates. The Jews pour out their hearts at the wailing wall. Moslems bow their heads and prostrate themselves at the Mosque of Omar. Christians walk in solemn procession on the Via Dolorosa, or weep at Gordon's Calvary, or inspire their souls as they stand in the garden of Gethsemane beneath the three-thousand-year-old olive trees, which apparently witnessed the agony of the Saviour as He bowed low in prayer in their shade, when the shadow of the cross was over Him. There is another locality, the Church of the Holy Sepulcher, which is spoken of as the place of our Lord's crucifixion. There is much uncertainty, however, as to whether the wall of Jerusalem in His time excluded or included this area.

The Temple Area and Western Wall

There is an elevation north of the city, Mount Scopus, and if from there you look east and south you see more than just a valley before you, for the mountains seem to sink away over the Judean desert, and down very low to the Dead Sea and Jericho. From this point you can observe the eastern wall of the city, and the temple area with the shining golden Dome of the Rock. Below, you can see that the gate in the eastern wall, known as the Golden Gate, is still closed and sealed, even built up, until the coming of Messiah, as the Jews would have all to understand.

The beauty of the Mount Morah temple area will strike you; not only is there the golden dome, but also there are lawns and cyprus trees covering about thirty-five acres, nearly a mile in circumference. At the far side of this enclosure is the western wall of Herod's temple. Until just after the six-day war there were Arab dwellings in close proximity to the wall, although outside the temple area, but these were soon bulldozed away to give visitors a better view of the wall. Pilgrims can now come more easily and stand back and wonder as they take advantage of the wider view, but it is the Jews who still come to pray and make request to Jehovah for their brethren scattered over the earth, and for His blessing on the city. Undoubtedly there is a burning desire in many a Jew's heart for the rebuilding of the temple itself. Today they can be seen placing in every little crevice between the great stones scraps of paper on which they have written prayers for the prosperity of Jerusalem and for its peace. They undoubtedly recall what David said: "They shall prosper that love thee."

The division through the heart of the city of Jerusalem lasted nearly twenty years, but no longer exists. Between 1948 and the six-day war this border drew nearer the western limits, but still remained right through the city, producing a narrow no-man's-land, with dead-end alleys, scars of recurring battles, mine fields, and half-demolished blackened buildings with twisted girders. Today there is very little sign in the actual city of all these past problems when old Jerusalem was in Arab hands and separated firmly from the new part of the city on the western side. Only in respect to its inhabitants is there any semblance of a division in Jerusalem today, and that may not be too noticeable to the ordinary tourist. There is the Jewish quarter of the city, the Christian quarter, and Moslem and Armenian sections, too.

Quite near to the Armenian quarter, there is David's citadel, from the top of which one can see much of the city. Several gates are discernable from this position, such as the Damascus and Jaffa gates and others made famous by the Bible records.

David's Mount Zion

Just outside the wall of old Jerusalem, on the south side, is Mount Zion, the site of David's original city, with the traditional place of the institution of the Lord's Supper, the upper room. But from Mount Zion looking north and northwest you can see the new part of Jerusalem (not the Biblical New Jerusalem which is above) with its modern buildings. There is the Knesset which holds the Israeli government, and the Israel Museum, the Shrine of the Book, which holds the Dead Sea scrolls. The Hebrew University (which has twelve thousand students) and the YMCA building are also in this area. Further west on Mount Hersal is the Hersal museum, which honors the memory of the founder of Zionism.

A few miles out of Jerusalem, you can still see the fields beside Bethlehem, where the shepherds kept their flocks by night nearly two thousand years ago. This is the city from which Naomi departed to go with her husband to Moab, and the place to which she returned with her

Moabitess daughter-in-law. Ruth here met Boaz, a mighty man of wealth, a kinsman of Naomi, who became Ruth's redeemer and husband, and an important link in the line of our Redeemer, the Messiah Jesus. As today you look over to Bethlehem you seem to hear the angels praising, as they did on that memorable night when Jesus was born, born to die to redeem mankind, "born of a woman, born under the Law, in order that He might redeem those who were under the Law" (Galatians 4:4-5).

Old Jerusalem today is very cosmopolitan, comparable in this respect, at least, to the city of New York. People from every land and tongue and nation and religion meet here, and meet they must if they come to these narrow streets and winding stairways in and around Jerusalem. It is true that many changes have come to parts outside the city walls; suburbs with modern buildings surround the city, especially on the western side. But within the walls little, it seems, has changed since Herod ruled here and Caiaphas the high priest fulfilled his functions, and Jesus of Nazareth walked along these stony streets and talked of the glory coming His way. "But first," He said, "He must suffer many things and be rejected by this generation" (Luke 17:25)! X

There seems to be little progress towards the internationalization of the city, as some have strongly advocated. The Jews believe it is their city today, and in reality has always been theirs, since King David captured it from the Jebusites. The Israeli government has declared Jerusalem nonnegotiable, and they believe now that it will remain theirs forever, as they repeatedly affirm. There are Jews in Jerusalem and Palestine from sixty or seventy countries of the world. This unique city is not only the capital of Israel, it is looked upon as the capital of all the millions of Jewish people around the world.

But the Jews are forced to rub shoulders day by day with the Arabs in the city, and their government has promised not only to leave Arab refugees within their country's borders and in their towns, but to protect them in certain ways. Nevertheless, there are great problems associated with this cohabitation attempt, not because of the cultural differences, although they are many, but because of the political impasse, which is growing in intensity day by day. Riots in the city and riots on the west bank of the Jordan and riots for this reason and that, are the order of today; but political hatred abounding within the walls of the city of peace is the basic reason for the existing state of affairs.

Jerusalem Reborn But Not Yet Redeemed

All this will undoubtedly show that old Jerusalem may be reborn but it is certainly not yet redeemed. It must be clearly understood by the Christian reader that this situation in Jerusalem today is not at all the work of Jehovah. It is not today that God is fulfilling His prophetic Word and dealing again in blessing with His ancient people (but of course, that day will certainly come). No! the Jews are returning to Israel in unbelief at this time. By the vast majority of them Jesus Christ is still rejected; by a great number even the God of their fathers is disowned or neglected. During this present age, therefore, God is not dealing with the Jews in any special way. God's chronometer for this chosen people is stopped, but it will start again. His covenants to Abraham and to David are unconditional and must be fulfilled.

Two things stand out clearly today. First, it is

Zionism, not Jehovah, which for many years has been opening up the way for Jews from around the world to return to Palestine. It is true that there has been some real success, but in 1975 it was reported that approximately 2,000 more Jews left Israel than arrived there. Secondly, things will be supremely different when the Lord Himself regathers Jews to their own land. It is evident that there has been no fulfillment as yet of such prophecies as the following: "Then you shall dwell in the land which I have given to you and to your forefathers" (Jeremiah 35:15) and "Behold, the days are coming . . . When I [will] raise up for David a righteous Branch; And He will reign as king. . . . In His days Judah will be saved, And Israel will dwell securely" (Jeremiah 23:5-6).

It is true that over two million Jews, encouraged by Zionism, have come to the land, but it is also obvious that they do not dwell in safety today and they are not enjoying rest from all their enemies. In sympathizing with them in their troubles, and in trying to understand the aspirations and difficulties of both Jews and Arabs, we must still wait on Almighty God to work out His will in His own way and in His own time. Before the blessing, however, will come the sifting and judging; before the redeeming must come the repentance and the mourning.

On October 21, 1976, the following came from Reporter Michael Elkins in Jerusalem: "During all the 28 years that Israel has been an independent state its national existence has been under threat. The Israelis have never known what fate awaits them around the next corner of time. . . . Whatever the future holds is in the future and thus unknowable, and for Israelis the present is difficult enough, and it is all they can deal with."

Zionism in Jerusalem today is interpreted to mean

different things. There are some who think that Zionism means simply the regathering and returning of Jews from exile around the world. For those Jews who are finding life most trying in the countries where they dwell, this view is predominant. For others, Zionism is a political movement to reestablish the Jews as a nation in the land of Israel to serve them with a center for cultural development, and to care for their welfare. Still others believe (and many significantly are found in Jerusalem) that it has to be a religious movement, for they interpret it as the answer to the prayers of Jews for centuries that their homeland and Jerusalem have been reborn. Three times a day the observant Jew has prayed for this; at the Passover seder and at their marriage ceremonies this has been the request. Those who look upon it as a religious movement expect that from it will arise a nation, built upon principles of social justice with practical and ethical standards, which will be a demonstration of the teachings of the Hebrew prophets and traditions, which they hope will produce spiritual inspiration to all the world.

It is true to say that the orthodox are not all of the same mind about Zionism. Some of them assert that only a Messiah could redeem the nation of Israel, while others are pleased to find in this an answer to their prayers and real hope for the future.

Officially Zionism had its birth in 1897, but there was never any general agreement as to its main purpose. Through it some wanted refuge in Israel for Jews who were being oppressed in their own lands; others saw in it a rebirth of the Hebrew language and a revival of Jewish culture; and religious Jews have believed for years that in having a homeland many of their brethren would adhere more strictly to the rituals of their ancient faith.

The recent prime minister of Israel, General Yitzhak Rabin, has his roots in Zionism. He was born in the city of Jerusalem of Zionist parents from Russia. During the six-day war of June 1967 Rabin was commander of the forces which captured old Jerusalem, and in doing so he fulfilled his life's dream and ambition. Rabin is a born soldier. In 1956 he was given control of the northern command, and for some twenty-seven years has had a brilliant military career. In 1948, when the British mandate ended, he threw back the Arab forces with less than a million people from which to draw. So it was in 1967 his plans as chief of staff, together with General Dayan in the field, led Israel to victory, in what is now known as the six-day war. Rabin became the Israeli ambassador to the United States in 1968. The Yom Kippur war in 1973 at first took Israel by surprise, as apparently there was some human error in the analysis of information received at the time. The setback, however, was only temporary, and this in itself became the inspiring motive for greater alertness. In 1974, within six months of Rabin entering politics, he was made prime minister. Little progress toward a Middle East peace settlement was made during his period of office, and in 1977 some legal irregularities regarding a bank account he and his wife maintained in the United States forced his resignation.

In the election that followed in the late spring of the same year, the three million Jews in Israel showed their real attitude about holding on to the west bank area and their survival in the land, choosing Menachem Begin to be their leader. With the help of two smaller religious groups he was able to form a coalition government. Begin, also a Zionist, was born in Poland. He is known to be tough and to possess hawkish tendencies, but nevertheless is already finding that he must make certain modifications to his promises because of the present uneasy situation.

Of the people now inhabiting Jerusalem, 75 per cent are Jews. They are witnessing this city achieving greatness once more. They rejoice that it has become the hub of the Jewish state and the admiration of world Jewry.

Concerning the Jews' Return

Some students of prophecy attempt to show that the sections of Scripture to which we have referred concerning the return of the Jews to Palestine (i.e., "you shall dwell in the land"), were completely fulfilled in their return under Ezra in 539 B.C. But then, we must note, was it not from Babylon that they returned at that time, and not from the four quarters of the earth, as the Prophet Isaiah affirms? "In that day . . . the nations will resort to the root of Jesse, Who will stand as a signal for the peoples; And His resting place will be glorious. . . . [and] the Lord will assemble the outcasts of Israel, and gather together the dispersed of Judah from the four corners of the earth" (Isaiah 11:10-12).

The same context plainly states that this is to be a second return and there has been no second return up to this present time. When they do return for a second time, they are to be established in the land forever.

There are other students of prophecy who suggest that Israel has forfeited all rights and expectations for a return as we outline here, because of her unbelief and above all because of her rejection of Christ. However, this disobedience by Israel and her unfaithfulness generally is not only foreseen by the prophets, but the same writers speak of their return to their own land and of their eventual acceptance by God when they accept their Messiah. If therefore their unfaithfulness has been clearly established, yet God remains faithful to His covenant, He cannot deny Himself. "He will again have compassion on us . . . Thou wilt give truth to Jacob and unchanging love to Abraham, Which Thou didst swear to our forefathers From the days of old" (Micah 7:19-20).

Earlier Jehovah Himself speaks through the prophet and declares that the very same people to whom He brought affliction, He will regather and be King over them in Zion. "In that day . . . I will assemble the lame, and gather the outcasts, Even those whom I have afflicted. I will make the lame a remnant, And the outcasts a strong nation, And the LORD will reign over them in Mount Zion From now on and forever" (Micah 4:6-7).

The method of God's dealing with Israel is clearly seen in this passage. First, He afflicted her in righteousness and cast her off. Then, He promises He will gather her, assemble her, make of her a strong nation, and reign over her Himself forever, and that will be in Jerusalem. "Shout for joy, O daughter of Zion! . . . Rejoice . . . O daughter of Jerusalem! . . . I will . . . gather the outcast, And I will turn their shame into praise and renown in all the earth" (Zephaniah 3:14,19).

Those who have been a curse among the nations will be a blessing to them, shame will be turned to praise, but only when Israel is regathered to her own land by the Lord God Himself. "Behold, I am going to save My people from the land of the east and from the land of the west; and I will bring them back, and they will live in the midst of Jerusalem, and they will be My people and I will be their God. . . . Just as you were a curse among the nations . . . so I will save you [so] that you may become a blessing. . . . I have again purposed in these days to do good to Jerusalem (Zechariah 8:1-15). These are encouraging words for despised Jews: "Praise and fame in every land," but without doubt they must be for fulfillment in the future, for there has never been known such an attitude to the Jew, as is described here.

There is another school of thought among prophetic students, that all these prophecies are being fulfilled in the history of the Church. This fanciful spiritualizing, ascribing literally all the curses to the Jews and all the blessings to the Church, is noticeably inconsistent in its exegesis of Scripture, doing violence to the laws of Biblical interpretation. For instance, these accept the first half of a single verse in Micah's prophecy as being literally fulfilled at our Lord's first coming, but the second half of the same verse is spiritualized to apply in some way to the Church (Micah 5:2). These prophecies here speak of the land directly (that is, Judah and Palestine) and Jerusalem itself, of the reign of David's seed from this city, and of the prosperity of that reign with agricultural developments and produce in plenty.

On the other hand it is not the Church which is being brought back to God. She is not a company of His original people who had wandered away. The Church rather is a called-out assembly of sinners saved by grace. It is true that sinners are brought from spiritual death to life, upon their reception of Christ, but who would be so naive as to identify this with a migration from all over the world to Palestine?

We must keep our eyes on Jerusalem and the nation of Israel, and at the same time make an attempt rightly to divide the prophecies about them in the Word. In the end of this age events will move more quickly than ever before as God uses human strategy to fulfill His Word and man's planning to praise Him. His promises to His ancient people will come to pass, in spite of differing opinions and varying interpretations. The situation today certainly gives them hope, and must give to the Christian a keener interest in the Lord's return. To mention a few signs most prominent: the nation of Israel is homeless no more; the city of Jerusalem is trodden down by the Gentiles no more; the desert is blossoming as the rose again; and Jerusalem is again becoming the center of the earth. The stage is being set at the crossroads of the world, not only for an ever-increasingly powerful nation of Israel to be reckoned with, but for the greatest conflagration in the history of the world to take place, the battle of Armageddon. A spiritually decadent Israel has yet to answer to her God. Jerusalem will yet repent and say: "Blessed is He that cometh in the name of the Lord," and we can surely "see the day approaching."

The Scriptures clearly indicate that the fulfillment of these prophecies will commence in earnest after the Church has been removed from this scene by being caught up suddenly to meet the Lord in the air (1 Thessalonians 4). The man of sin will then appear on the scene and among the wonders he will perform, by the power of Satan, will be the securing of peace in the Middle East by the signing of an agreement with Israel for a period of seven years. Then it will be, with peace guaranteed, Jews from all over the world will flock by tens of thousands to Israel, and in this way God Himself will recommence His special dealings with His ancient chosen people.

Because, however, God is holy in all His works and ways, He must in all righteousness deal with them in judgment before He can save them in grace. The second half of this time of judgment, a period of some three-and-a-half years, is spoken of in the Scripture as the great tribulation, or the time of Jacob's trouble. It will commence when the man of sin, who will virtually be a world ruler by this time, will break the covenant he has made with the Jews: "When they shall say 'peace and safety!' then destruction will come upon them suddenly" (1 Thessalonians 5:3). During the tribulation, judgment will come to all the earth, but in particular to Israel.

Although today Israel possesses her homeland, and Jerusalem its capital, both city and nation wait uneasily, wondering who, when, where, and what will strike next.

Michael Elkins, reported from Jerusalem in October 1976 (immediately following the Arab agreement to police Lebanon and enforce a cease-fire in that country's bitter civil war): "It is taken as axiomatic in Israel that Syrian influence over Lebanon will be maintained and will be decisive, that in the future Lebanon will become what Syria wants it to become. . . . Other Israeli leaders believe Syria has moved to control Lebanon and the PLO [Palestine Liberation Organization] in order to be able to open a new front against Israel along the Lebanese border, and to ensure that this will happen when (when, not if) Syria is ready for war."

Jerusalem Yesterday and Today

Yesterday she rejected her Messiah and King, but today the Jews need a deliverer as in the time of the judges. Tomorrow, they will need no one less than the Son of God, to save them from the nations of the earth gathered against them. Glorious will be the day when He who does come will come as their Deliverer and King.

Yesterday the streets of the city of Jerusalem flowed with blood when Titus in A.D. 70 slaughtered the inhabitants and those who tried to escape. Today, in the last quarter of the twentieth century, Jerusalem is reborn and the streets are flowing with pilgrims and sightseers and vendors and guides and police.

Yesterday, the Jews lost their national independence and their city was trodden down by the Gentiles for centuries. Today, Jerusalem is the capital of an independent Israeli state, it is an ever-expanding city in an apparently ever-expanding nation.

Yesterday, the Jews were hounded from their city and they poured out from its gates in despair, to suffer privation through their dispersion around the world. Today, the gates of the city are open wide, and through them Jews freely enter Jerusalem, drawn by an inherent longing to be back home, and encouraged by Zionism to build up the city and develop the land.

Yesterday, it seemed that the city of Jerusalem had been obliterated, that Jewish nationhood had perished, and that the doom prophesied by the major and minor prophets of the Old Testament had been literally fulfilled (but observe the rays of light and hope which shine at the conclusion of these prophecies). Today, there is a revival of Jewish nationhood, and the capital of Israel is not only beautiful for situation, but resplendent with its ancient buildings and modern amenities, an attraction to people of all races and religions from all parts of the earth.

Yesterday, the Hebrew language seemed on the way out, for it was quite natural and even wise for Jews dispersed abroad to use the language of the country of their adoption, though a tragic blow to their national pride. Today, the Hebrew language is not only taught in Jewish schools but generations of Israelis are now arising who speak freely and always in their old mother tongue.

Yesterday, the land was barren, the city bare, and the inhabitants poor; there was hardship on every hand and a grim struggle for survival. Today, there is prosperity in this new industrious state; there are collective farms on the land, and a new type of communal living and working, the *kibbutz*, which is very successful, making a marked rise in the standard of living.

Yesterday, they were overcome by the armies of their enemies from the north, the walls of the city broken down, and the Temple burned with fire. Today, there is a strong and efficient army with the most modern weapons to protect the beloved city and the Israeli nation.

Yesterday, they were forced to vacate their homeland and their city as destruction poured down upon them. Today, there is a revival of their ancestral home, history has repeated itself once more, with Jerusalem being rebuilt and extended and becoming the home of thousands of Jews.

Yesterday, when small groups of Jews returned to visit the city, they were not welcome, and indeed were sometimes attacked in violence. Today, there is a marked increase in the Jewish population, especially in the urban areas around Jerusalem itself; Jews usually make up the welcoming committee for pilgrims from abroad, and they themselves are the guides.

Today the state of Israel is open to the immigration of Jews from all countries of their dispersion, and the inhabitants of both city and country are benefiting from the general development. The principles for governing the nation are based upon liberty, justice, and peace, as conceived by the prophets of old. There is said to be political equality for all citizens, without distinction of religion, race, or sex, and the aim is freedom of religion, conscience, education, and culture. The holy places of all religions are safeguarded, especially in and around the old city of Jerusalem.

The ideals of the state of Israel set out above are similar to and based upon the Declaration of Independence. They are sufficiently noble and good, but how far they can be implemented, when pressures build up against her, remains to be seen. However, a day will surely come when there will be equity and peace, when "a king [shall] reign righteously" (Isaiah 32:1).

7

JERUSALEM PREPARES FOR HER KING

For both the Jew and Jerusalem, there is to be a great future. Some have feared, especially during recent Middle East wars, that the two-and-a-half million Jews and their small state would be eventually overrun by the one hundred million Arabs of the neighboring countries. Everyone must now see the obvious trends in the opposite direction. With these and the increasing might in modern weaponry of this still very small state, many are wondering if God Himself is not, after all, controlling events to prepare for a complete fulfillment of all the prophecies about the Jews, their city, and their homeland.

Although God is not dealing specifically with the Jews at this time, and His actual working in them and for them will not recommence until the Church has been taken away, yet He is certainly overruling the events among the nations and preparing the Jews in many ways for His future dealings with them, first in chastisement and then in blessing.

God is using Zionism to prepare, not only His ancient people, but also their city for the time when the suspension of His dealings with them is lifted. He is preparing the land of Palestine, and even the earth beneath their feet, for a momentous day in the not too distant future, when He shall come whose right it is to reign and His feet shall stand upon the Mount of Olives. The geological fault, now known to exist under Olivet, will become active and the hill will divide asunder at that precise moment, leaving a great new valley.

The stage in the Middle East and in Jerusalem itself is being set for the resumption of God's dealings with the Jews. There have been five events which themselves are prominent signs of this trend. As early as 1791 there was the removal of all exceptional laws against the Jews by the French National Assembly, and Jewish influence was soon observed in both high finance and politics. There was the founding of Zionism in 1897, with its influence on suffering Jews around the world to return to Palestine. The Balfour declaration was signed in 1917 with part of Palestine being declared a national home for the Jews under British protection. The climax was the founding of the Jewish state in independence in 1948.

The Times of the Gentiles

Of course, the liberating of the old city of Jerusalem during the six-day war in 1967 was of great significance for Jews and for Christians, too. Some students of prophecy immediately saw in this the end of the times of the Gentiles, mainly because of the words of our Lord, "Jerusalem will be trampled underfoot by the Gentiles until the times of the Gentiles be fulfilled" (Luke 21:24). Our Lord was referring there to God's prophetic plan for Gentile world powers, as He gave it both to Nebuchadnezzar through his dream, and to Daniel in his interpretation of it. These times commenced with Nebuchadnezzar and the captivity of Judah and will end with the battle of Armageddon and the final deliverance of the Jews and their city by the coming in power and glory of the Son of God. The Gentile nations will be judged and the kingdom of Christ will be set up following His divine intervention. Jerusalem, at that time, will be finally and completely liberated, which suggests very strongly that the agonies of the Jews and their beloved city are not yet completely over.

However, the results of the six-day war were dramatic, to say the least, and the freeing of Jerusalem from Gentile power after nearly 2,000 years was a dynamic achievement for the Israelis. On only three brief occasions since the Babylonian destruction of Jerusalem in B.C. 587 did the Jews have absolute control of their city. In May 142 B.C. Judas Maccabeus removed the yoke of the Gentiles from Israel until the Roman occupation of Jerusalem in 63 B.C. Then there was the repudiation of Caesar's overlordship of the Temple and the city in A.D. 66, which lasted until the Roman conquest again in 70 A.D. The third period was from the outbreak of the second Jewish revolt, led by Barkokhba in 132, until its reduction by the Romans three years later.

Back Home in Jerusalem

Immediately following the liberation of Jerusalem in June 1967, Premier Eskol stood in the city, near to the wailing wall, and made a proclamation: "I send greetings of peace to our Jewish brethren wherever they be. Blessed be He who has kept us alive and enabled us to reach this hour."

Then Michael Elkins asked Sergeant Meier Wassermann of Tiberias, who had led his men triumphantly into the old city and to the wall, how he felt. His reply was impressive: "Reporter," he said, "Put it down like this: I, me, myself, feel that I have come home after 2,000 years" (*Newsweek,* June 19, 1967).

It is well known that three times a day an orthodox Jew prays (in the Eighteen Benedictions): ". . . and return speedily to Jerusalem, Thy city, in mercy and dwell within, as Thou hast spoken."

One Amos Oz said (as reported in *The Seventh Day,* by Andre Deutsch): "Now Jerusalem was different, it had begun to live again. . . . Hosts of pious Jews, soldiers in battle dress, amazed tourists, all streamed eastwards. . . . The Bible came to life for me, the prophets, the kings, the temple mount, and Absalom's pillar, and I wanted to be part of it all." Another soldier, Eliezer, is recorded as saying: "I asked a fellow soldier what he thought of it all. He answered, 'I was glad when they said unto Me, "Let us go into the House of the Lord. Our feet shall stand within Thy gates, O, Jerusalem" ' . . . When we broke into the old city and I went up to the temple mount and later to the western wall, I looked at the officers and soldiers. I saw their tears, and I knew they felt as I did . . . in my pocket there was a book of Psalms written by David, the King of Jerusalem."

This nation went to war in 1967 with a sense of destiny. Not only did they make history militarily and fulfill Jewish yearnings symbolically, but they were beginning to fulfill prophecy literally. This march into the old city was just as significant as the war of independence. Then the state was born, but in 1967 Jerusalem was reborn; then they found their home, but in conquering the old city they found their heart. This was the high point of the war, and the Jews who entered the city did not talk, or even pray, they stood and wept and sang between their sobs, "Jerusalem the Golden."

The Jerusalem government was taken by surprise

a few years later at the time of the Yom Kippur war, modern Israel's fourth. It was Saturday, October 6, 1973, that the attacks were made on Israel, on the Egyptian and Syrian fronts. The greatest tank battle of all times transpired in the desert of Sinai on Friday, October 19. The Egyptians alone had 3,000 tanks, and there were as many or more on the Syrian front as in the offensive against Russia by the German Nazis in 1941. The prime minister, Golda Meir, was heard to confess shortly afterwards, "For the first time in our twenty-five years' history, we thought we might have lost." There are many who feel that the salvation of Israel at this time was a direct intervention of God, but God will not deal directly with Israel until the Church is removed. But no doubt the stage is being set in the Middle East for the final conflagration.

Another traumatic scare for Israel came soon after the unofficial cease-fire of the Yom Kippur war. The cease-fire was broken several times by the Egyptians, and finally Israel decided to push them back. So successful was this thrust, that they reached a place within fifty miles of Cairo. Russia decided she must intervene, and announced in a cable to President Nixon that she planned to take unilateral action against Israel. Huge transport planes and regiments of crack Soviet parachutists were ready to take off from Russia to the Middle East; a large Soviet warship with ballistic missiles and nuclear warheads had already docked at Alexandria. But Nixon ordered a worldwide United States military alert, putting well over two million men on stand-by. Russia did not proceed with its threat, world war three was avoided, Israel was saved again, and Jerusalem was preserved once more.

Jerusalem today is crowded with Jews and, though

perhaps unconsciously, they are being prepared for a coming great event, unprecedented and stupendous. They will welcome their King from Heaven, as the risen Christ, after they have suffered further tribulation. Even the land of Israel is being prepared for a time of bounty and blessing. It is becoming amazingly fertile again, and beginning to blossom as the rose. Already the land is productive agriculturally, with annual rainfall over twenty-six inches.

Twelve Tribes to Be in the Land

There are well over two-and-a-half million Jews in Israel. God is beginning to fulfill His Word even through the efforts of Zionism, for He will use whomsoever and whatsoever He wills in His sovereignty to perform His own purposes. Nevertheless, there must be some little way still to go before we see the fulfillment of such prophecies as this: "In those days the house of Judah will walk with the house of Israel, and they will come together from the land of the north to the land that I gave to your fathers as an inheritance" (Jeremiah 3:18). There is a prediction here that there will be twelve tribes in the land in that day! "I will again have compassion on them; and I will bring them back, each one to his inheritance and each one to his land" (Jeremiah 12:15).

Ezekiel corroborates God's promise given through Jeremiah: "For I will take you from the nations, gather you from all the lands, and bring you into your own land" (Ezekiel 36:24). Notice it is Jehovah who says, "I will bring you," and when He does it, the efforts of Zionism will pale into insignificance. Once more He adds, "In the latter years you shall come into the land that is brought back from the sword . . . and they shall dwell safely all of them" (Ezekiel 38:8 KJV). Real safety with no threatening sword is promised for the Jews by Jehovah.

More Signs Appear

The spirit of lawlessness throughout the world today must also be a pointer that we are in the last days of this age when "that lawless one will be revealed . . . whose coming is in accord with the activity of Satan . . . with . . . signs and false wonders" (2 Thessalonians 2:8-9). This man of sin, as he is named in Paul's second letter to the Thessalonians, is not yet revealed, but there is evidence on every hand that the world is preparing for his coming with the spread of lawlessness (he is the lawless one), not only on the campuses of colleges and in factories, but even in homes and in the streets.

World economic crises and insolvable problems of international finance and food supplies suggest that man is already coming towards the end of his day. Gentile power among the nations must soon give way to the rule of God's King, and the inauguration of God's day in the earth.

This is man's day. He is having his way in the world, but it must certainly end in catastrophe, for man without God in God's world is doomed to failure. The times of the Jews ended in captivity through their infidelity, and the times of the Gentiles, which commenced at that period, will end with their collapse at the appearance of Christ, as foretold in the prophetic Scriptures. This will be the dawning of God's day, in which He will have His way in His earth, through the rule of His King (God's day as opposed to man's day—not the "Day of God" here).

God's day will commence with the coming of the King with ten thousand of His saints, So this must be preceded by His coming for His saints.

In God's day the Church will share Christ's glorious reign, So this must be preceded by a resurrection and a rapture.

In God's day Jerusalem will become the capital of Christ's reign, So this must be preceded by her final deliverance from Gentile oppression.

In God's day there will be salvation and blessing for Israel, So this must be preceded by divine chastisement and Israel's repentance.

In God's day there will be peace among the nations, So this must be preceded by a judgment of the nations.

In God's day the adversary will be powerless, So this must be preceded by the binding of Satan.

In God's day His covenants will be completely fulfilled, So this must be preceded by a complete control of Palestine by the Jews, their complete acceptance of Christ as Messiah and King, and His complete dominion over the earth, for "All the earth will be filled with the glory of the LORD" (Numbers 14:21).

The amalgamation of many religious systems has begun, and will certainly develop, with the help of the World Council of Churches, until there is a final heading up under the religious head who is the false prophet. This will occur during Jerusalem's short period of peace, which itself will be shattered by the demands of the man of sin, and the refusal of the Jews to worship him. It has been difficult to envisage so-called Christian and other religions of the world becoming united under a Jewish religious leader, but Christians today worship a Jewish Saviour, and people who remain after His coming will accept the false prophet, who is antichrist, who will come in his own name.

Another shadow moving across our path these days is the current trend towards the occult and world interest in spirits and Satan worship. These are warnings of dark days of trial ahead when the trinity of evil—the man of sin, the false prophet, and Satan himself—join to deceive mankind with their sorceries, witchcraft, and lying wonders. The apostle predicts this: "In the latter times . . . some shall depart from the faith, giving heed to seducing spirits, and doctrines of devils; Speaking lies in hypocrisy" (1 Timothy 4:1 KJV).

The King Is Coming

Nothing short of an intervention by God will be sufficient to curb the onslaughts of evil, and to save Jerusalem from Gentile powers in their bid to conquer Palestine. Just as "when the fulness of . . . time came, God sent forth His son . . . that He might redeem" (Galatians 4:4), so God will once more in a literal way fulfill His promises by sending Christ from His side to deliver and restore Jerusalem and her people.

We now conclude that although the liberation of Jerusalem in 1967 was one of Israel's greatest achievements since the time of the Maccabees, her hold onto the city, no matter how determined she might be, cannot be permanent as yet. The words of the Saviour are still for future fulfillment, and Jerusalem will be delivered yet again in the day of the completion of the times of the Gentiles.

God is to be glorified in her refinement and chastisement; Christ is to be vindicated in the place of His rejection; Jerusalem is to be freed, finally, only by His coming in great power and glory.

8

JERUSALEM AT THE END OF THE CHURCH AGE

The past rejection of Christ, the soon-coming completion of the Church, and the final deliverance of Jerusalem are all outstanding events which signify the end of an age, and are deeply significant for the Jew, the Gentile, and the Church of God. When Christ was crucified, the accusation over His head on the cross was written in Hebrew, Greek, and Latin, suggesting that all the known world had a share in His rejection: the religious Jews, the refined Greeks, and the ruling Romans. But God's plan was far from being finished. He raised His Son from the dead and Christ ascended on high, to be made King of Glory. Actually all authority was given to Him, not only in Heaven, but on the earth also. It is therefore His right to reign over the earth now, but it is not yet His time to do so. The purpose of all prophecy, however, is to reveal how and when God will vindicate His Son and see that He receives authority and glory in the very place of His rejection, the city of Jerusalem, and throughout the earth.

In the meantime it is the divine purpose, as foreseen by Christ Himself, to call out from the world a people for His name, those who trust His Son. This is the mystery (a sacred secret now made known to believers) spoken of by the Apostle Paul: "That the Gentiles are fellow-heirs and fellow-members of the body, and fellow-partakers of the promise in Christ Jesus through the gospel" (Ephesians 3:6). This called-out company is likened to a building: "Having been built upon the foundation of the apostles and prophets, Christ Jesus Himself being the cornerstone, in whom the whole building, groweth unto a holy temple in the Lord" (Ephesians 2:20-21).

When this mystic building, the Church of God on earth, is complete (and this is the objective of all true evangelistic programs—not to convert the world but to complete the Church), then it will be purposeless for the Church to remain on earth. The Father will send the Son from Heaven to gather His own to Himself. This act is, in itself, the answer to our Lord's high priestly prayer: "Father, I desire that they also, whom Thou hast given Me, be with Me where I am" (John 17:24), and it is a fulfillment of His promise to His own: "I will come again, and receive you to Myself; that where I am, there you may be also" (John 14:3).

When our Lord has thus completed the Church through His servants on earth and has called her away from the world into His own presence, the work of God in chastising and judging Israel, His ancient, erring people, will commence. All this will be their preparation by Jehovah for the time when His unique Son will reign from their city as King over all the earth.

The Church to Be "Caught Up"

The calling away of the Church, the company of true believers, into the heavens to meet the Lord is the next great unprecedented happening for this planet earth.

"Summoned away the children of day, Left the children of night." This distinction is seen clearly in 1 Thessalonians 5:2-10: "The day of the Lord [His coming in judgment] will come just as a thief in the night. While they [Israel and the world] are saying, 'Peace and safety!' then destruction will come upon them suddenly. . . . But you, brethren [the Church], are not in darkness, that the day should overtake you . . . you are all sons of light and sons of day. . . . For God has not destined us for wrath, but for obtaining salvation . . . that . . . we . . . may live together with Him.''

This salvation is the rapture, the first stage of our Lord's second coming, the completion of the salvation which believers have in Him. The contrast is clear. Christians are children of the day—the day of Christ—and not children of darkness, nor appointed to wrath at the Day of the Lord, which is the second stage of His coming.

The Two Stages of Christ's Second Coming

At the first stage it will be the Lord Himself, the Saviour who will appear; at the second stage He will come as the Son of Man.

At the first stage He will come for the Church's rapture; at the second stage He will come to deliver Israel.

At the first stage He will come to the air; at the second stage He will come to the earth.

At the first stage He will come for His saints; at the second stage He will come with His saints.

At the first stage He will appear without sin unto salvation; at the second stage He will appear to take vengeance on His enemies.

At the first stage His own will be taken to be forever with the Lord; at the second stage the ungodly will be taken for judgment.

At the first stage He will come in the twinkling of an

eye and secretly; at the second stage He will come publicly and every eye shall see Him.

At the first stage He will raise those who have died
in Him; at the second stage there will be no resurrection.

At the first stage the trumpet of God will sound; at
the second stage the angel's trumpet will sound.

At the first stage He will appear as the Morning
Star; at the second stage He will appear as the Sun of
Righteousness.

Details of the first stage were given by special revelation; details of the second stage were the subject of
prophecy.

The first stage is called the Day of Christ; the second
stage is the Day of the Lord.

When the Church therefore is caught up, or snatched
away, the heavenly Bridegroom will receive His bride;
believers will receive their rewards; the people left on
earth will receive the tribulations foretold in detail in
the book of Revelation; the Jews will receive the judgments of God in the time known as "Jacob's trouble,"
and Jerusalem will receive double for all her sins.

If at the second stage of our Lord's second coming
He will appear with the thousands of His saints, then at
the first stage there must be both a resurrection and a
rapture, and these two are inseparable and instanta-
neous according to 1 Thessalonians 4. He must first
come for His saints, if later He is to come with them.

God's chronometer, in relation to His dealings with
Jerusalem and the Jews, will be restarted immediately
following the rapture of the Church, and the final week
of the seventy weeks of years as announced by God to
Daniel with regard to his (Daniel's) people, the Jews, will
then begin. "Seventy weeks have been decreed for your

people and your holy city, to finish the transgression,
to make an end of sin, to make atonement for iniquity,
[and] to bring in everlasting righteousness" (Daniel 9:24).
Although the Hebrew word "weeks" simply means
"sevens," it is a period of seven years in question here,
evidenced by the fact that sixty-nine periods of seven
years transpired between the decree of Darius, king of
the Chaldeans, to rebuild the city of Jerusalem and the
crucifixion of Christ.

God's Seventieth Week for Daniel's People

This final seven-year period will commence with
Jerusalem and her people feeling secure. Peace will be
the order of the day. A covenant of peace will be signed
with the man of sin, or lawlessness, the first "beast" of
Revelation 13. This creature is of course a man, and he
will guarantee peace for seven years. It seems inevitable
therefore that Jerusalem will at that time welcome returning exiles in far greater numbers than ever before. This will
be the Lord's doing (not that of Zionism), His way of
bringing them once again to their land. Thus He will use
the man of sin to fulfill His purposes, just as He used the
ruthless Chaldeans many years ago to bring judgment to
Jerusalem. But just as the Chaldeans were eventually
brought to judgment themselves, so the doom of this
man of sin, the false prophet his compatriot, and even
Satan himself, is sure.

At the beginning of this time Jerusalem will be free
from Gentile domination, but the high hopes of world
Jewry, for the control of Jerusalem for all time, will be
dashed to the ground through the eventual breaking of
the covenant by the man of sin, the one who made it. The

ensuing bitter opposition to Israel by the ten-kingdom confederacy, of which the man of sin will be the political head, will invite the kings of the south and east to join in the general advance toward Jerusalem and Palestine, resulting in the battle of Armageddon, the escape of Jews to the wilderness, and finally a mighty deliverance for them and their city by the appearance of the Son of Man in power and glory.

Jerusalem may well be called the indestructible city, because although besieged, destroyed, and burned on so many occasions, it has arisen again and again, as though the secret hand of Omnipotence has kept back its utter and complete obliteration on every occasion. The law governing the interpretation of Scripture, and especially the principles of double reference and partial and complete fulfillment of prophecy, must surely find plenty of scope in respect to this ancient city, which originally belonged to and now again is in the control of God's chosen people, the Jews. Jerusalem has had an important part to play as the historical, religious, and most desirable city of the world in one age after another. In the end times, and in the age yet to come, there will still be an even more important role for this city to play in international affairs, starting sooner than we may think, if indeed it has not already commenced. There is to be for her, if the unrealized eschatology of Scripture be our guide, a time of very great suffering, more than Jerusalem has ever yet witnessed. This will be followed by a period of peace and prosperity to last at first for a thousand years. The details, as described for us in the pages of Holy Scripture, we shall attempt to discuss in later chapters.

9

JERUSALEM IN HER TIME OF JUDGMENT

Although judgment is said to be God's "strange work" (Isaiah 28:21), because of His righteous character and because of man's sin it is an essential work for the Almighty. God loves the sinner because He is love, but God judges the sin because He is righteous. He cannot clear those who remain guilty through their rejection of His Son, the Saviour provided by God the Father at such infinite cost. In Malachi's day the people of Jerusalem raised their hands to Heaven and in derision asked, "Where is the God of justice?" (Malachi 2:17) They soon learned that although sometimes the God of justice and judgment hides Himself or is silent, He is always beholding and even recording the transgressions of His creatures, so that He can deal justly with them when the day of grace is over and the day of reckoning arrives. Every man is to be "judged according to his works."

The first judgment of note was outside the wall of Jerusalem: Jesus the Son of God was judged by the Father; it was "the good pleasure" (that is, the perfect will) of Jehovah to bruise His Son. . . . "He hath put Him to grief" (Isaiah 53:10 KJV). The only explanation for this is seen in John 3:16: "For God so loved the world."

The judgment—and rewards—of the believer's life comes next in order and is still for future fulfillment. Later on, at the great and terrible day of the Lord, as Joel the prophet described, Christ, in the presence of

His brethren the Jews, will give judgment against some of the Gentile nations for opposing or ignoring His people, and these nations will go into everlasting punishment. Others, who have reacted favorably to the Jewish witnesses during the tribulation, will find a place on earth during His millennial reign. The judgment of the great white throne is the final one. The wicked dead will be raised by God to stand before Christ to be judged, not only according to the book of life, but according to their works.

This throne of judgment is said to be great, speaking of divine authority; and it is white, which reminds us of divine righteousness. The One who will sit upon it (Christ) will be the Divine Judge, and the dead will stand there, the great and the small, a manifestation of divine impartiality. They will stand before God, signifying divine justice, and the books—the divine records—will be opened. Another book will be produced, the book of life—the divine standard—and they will be judged according to their works, bringing divine retribution. Those condemned will die the second death, and this will surely mean divine sorrow, for, "As I live! declares the Lord GOD, I take no pleasure in the death of the wicked" (Ezekiel 33:11). This death will be in the lake of fire, spelling out divine punishment, the fire of divine wrath forever burning the guilty conscience of the Christ rejecter.

The one judgment we have omitted to mention until this point, will take place between Christ's coming for His saints and His appearance with His saints, that is, in the second half of the tribulation period. It will be the judgment of Jerusalem and the Jewish nation, the whole house of Israel, the twelve tribes in the land, and those still living in other parts of the world. This is when the man of sin will be the world ruler, and the false prophet will have been received in Jerusalem by the Jews, the one who will come in his own name.

Many details about this time of Jacob's trouble, the great tribulation, and the judgment of Israel are purposely given by inspiration in Revelation 6–18. The first part of this seven-year period will be marked by open rebellion against God, and also with noticeable progress towards a one-world government, a one-world monetary system, and a one-world religion. The stage will be rapidly set for the man of sin to appear, first as head of a ten-kingdom confederacy of western European nations, and then as a virtual world ruler. He will assume great authority because of his Satan-inspired wisdom and by initiating a peace program for the Middle East. A covenant will be signed between his forces (probably the strongest power on earth at that time) and the state of Israel.

God will use the signing of this covenant to encourage Jews around the world to return in tens of thousands to Israel. God's ancient people will therefore be assembled in fulfillment of those many prophecies about their regathering to their own land, to receive just judgment from the hand of God, before their repentance and final spiritual restoration. All twelve tribes of Israel, as named in Revelation 7, will be represented in Palestine during the tribulation period, the seventieth week of Daniel's prophecy. Jerusalem, the capital, will be the envy of the nations around, the prize to attract their attention and intervention. At the end of this present age of grace, when the Church has been removed from this earthly scene, she will receive her reward at the judgment seat of Christ; the people of earth will receive great tribulation; and the Jews will receive their judgment from God for all their sins, but especially for their rejection of the true Messiah.

In speaking of the coming of the Spirit, the Saviour said that He would "convict the world concerning sin . . . because they do not believe in Me" (John 16:8-9). The spirit of wickedness will be personified at this time by the man of sin. He will be empowered by Satan, and there will be then no restraint to his working. Christians with their restraining influence will be gone, and the Holy Spirit, who is the Divine Restrainer of evil, will have departed with the Church (as far as the residential aspect of His presence is concerned). There is no doubt that the spirit of wickedness in the earth would have far more influence today were it not for the gracious working of the Holy Spirit. The Restrainer of 2 Thessalonians 2 must of necessity be the Holy Spirit because He is evidently stronger than the man of sin, that wicked one. He is the One who has been restraining through the ages continuously, and His work is throughout the whole earth, so He must be omnipresent. The Saviour said that one of the special ministries of the Spirit when He came would be to restrain evil (John 16:7-11). This is the One who is to be "taken out of the way" (2 Thessalonians 2:7).

For many years now, there has been a diligent search for peace in the Middle East. The strategic importance of Palestine can never be overestimated. The problems between Arabs and Jews seem to be insurmountable, and present prospects of suitable solutions seem remote.

The political leader of the ten-kingdom confederacy, who shall arise after the rapture of the Church, will achieve notoriety for many reasons and for outstanding exploits, but none so impressive as that of making a peace covenant between his forces and the Jews; one which will be, if not altogether acceptable, generally accepted by the world rulers. This will be a seven-year guarantee of security and peace which this son of perdition will give to Israel, which itself will cause a cry of "Peace, peace, at last," to be heard around the world. But it is this same man of sin who will, in the middle of the allotted time, break the covenant he has formed.

A Counterfeit Trinity

The powers of evil will stalk across the earth, manifesting themselves in blasphemy, sorcery, immorality, and Satan worship to a degree not known before. Not only will unparalleled wickedness begin, but unparalleled judgment from God will commence, almost at the same time. There will be a trinity of evil, and a trinity of judgment. The seals of God's wrath will be broken, the trumpets of God's warnings will sound, and the bowls of God's righteous anger will be poured out. There is to be a trinity of sixes in the number of the name of the man of sin, and a trinity of cities prominent at this end time: Babylon, representing the false religion; old Jerusalem, representing the focal point of God's judgment for the Jews; and New Jerusalem, the dwelling place of the redeemed of the Lamb.

This will be followed by a trinity of nations or groups of nations who will gather against Palestine from west and south and east (most from the north will have been eliminated by this time). There will be a trinity of people: the sheep (some of the Gentile powers going on into the millennial reign), the goats (other Gentile nations going out into perdition), and "these brothers of Mine" (Matthew 25:40), as the Lord calls the remnant of the Jewish people, who will be saved and cleansed and share on earth some of the blessings of His reign through them.

The trinity of wickedness during the last half of the tribulation will be an attempt to counterfeit the divine Trinity. Satan will be thrust out of the first heaven, which is his domain ("the prince of the power of the air" he is called in Ephesians 2:2). Michael, the archangel of warfare, will cast him down to the earth, where he will arrive in person (but not in bodily form). His power and evil influence will become the tools of his emissaries, two men, who are described as two beasts in Revelation 13.

The first one mentioned is seen by John (Revelation 13:1) to have seven heads and ten horns and, we assume, arises out of the sea of Gentile nations. His ten horns, which are adorned with ten crowns, represent ten kings and so kingdoms, over which he rules with absolute authority. There is no Scripture to suggest that this man will be the Antichrist, for in fact the name antichrist does not appear in the book of Revelation, nor in Daniel's prophecy, and is never connected, in the places it is mentioned, with any figure of either history or prophecy. The Bible says there are many antichrists, and a dictionary is misleading if it applies this name to the great antagonist of the last days, the world dictator. This man of sin will be the political ruler of this tribulation period, and should be identified with that wicked person of 2 Thessalonians 2. The same ruler is mentioned several times in Daniel's prophecy.

The second beast mentioned in Revelation 13 is the false prophet, and he will certainly be antichrist in character, the religious ruler of the period. He will be received by Jews as well as by Christendom. John tells us that he arises out of the land, that is, Palestine, and so he will be a Jew. The marvel is that the one-world religious system by this time will be under his leadership. He is a false messiah but will be, nevertheless, accepted by most so-called Christian and religious organizations. At the beginning of August 1976 a united conference was held in Palestine between Jews and professing Christians. This amazing event will surely help us more easily to understand the prophesied Jewish leadership of a coming day. This false prophet will impersonate Christ, who is the true Prophet of God according to Moses and Stephen (see Acts 7:37), and if he is going to be anti-Christ, and Satan is going to be anti-God, then the man of sin will be anti-Spirit. These three persons will work as one, their power will have one source, that of Satan; and their purpose will be one also, to thwart the purpose of God in vindicating His Son in the earth.

The reign of the second beast, the religious ruler, will be from Jerusalem, and one of his main aims will be to see that the will of the man of sin is fulfilled in the Holy Land and in Jerusalem itself. He will deceive all earth dwellers, however, causing them to worship the man of sin. He will attempt to compel all the people of earth to receive the mark of the first beast (not his own mark) on their foreheads or on their right hands, and no one will be able to buy or sell without that mark—666, the number of the name of the man of sin.

The political head will come out of the sea of Gentile nations, and he is to be the man of sin, the world ruler. He will be lawless and oppose God and true religion. He will exalt himself as the object of worship, but his power will come from Satan. All Christ-rejecters will accept him, for "God will send upon them a deluding influence so that they might believe what is false" (2 Thessalonians 2:11). His end will be sure, however, and his doom certain. One of his confederate rulers will be wounded to death at the beginning, apparently in a power struggle, but he himself will intervene to raise him from the dead with the power given to him by the adversary.

This miracle (allowed by God, of course) will be an imitation of the greatest of all miracles, the raising of Christ from among the dead. It will cause the world to marvel at the beast and worship him the more, especially because of the peace he will bring to the Middle East, to Israel, and even to the world; but it is a peace which will not last. However he will go forth conquering and to conquer, receiving for some few years greater and greater authority, until the end of the first half of this seven-year judgment period.

Witnesses

God always has His witnesses. Before the cross, God's ancient people Israel were set apart to be His witnesses, but they sadly failed, and were set aside temporarily. After His resurrection our Lord said to His own, "You shall be My witnesses . . . to the remotest part of the earth" (Acts 1:8). Although there has been much failure on the part of Christians through the years, we praise the Lord for the efforts being made to fulfill the great commission and to witness for Christ, especially with the help of modern media techniques.

Following the Church's rapture there will be miracle conversions to God, similar perhaps to the one on the way to Damascus, when a great light from Heaven shone upon Saul of Tarsus, a chosen witness for Christ, opening the eyes of his soul to the truth as it is in Jesus. One hundred and forty-four thousand Jews, by a similar intervention of God, will see the truth (maybe acknowledging that evangelical Christians were right, evidenced by their sudden departure). They will be sealed by God as His property (sealing is always indicative of ownership) and they will be set aside to be His special witnesses throughout the world. Those who have heard the truth and rejected it will, of course, disregard them, except to torment them; but many of those who have never heard will be reached with the message of the kingdom of the coming King, the Messiah. These witnesses are spoken of as purchased from men out of the earth and will become the firstfruits to God and to the Lamb. They will form the first group prepared by their witnessing and testings to go on into the millennial reign of Christ over the earth. It should be noted that there are already Jews in Israel who can speak most of the languages of the world fluently, that is, the languages of the countries from which they have come.

Soon after the real judgment has begun, there will appear on the streets of Jerusalem two prophets of God, who will be His special witnesses to the world, not to bring the good news of the gospel, but an announcement of added judgments, plagues, and torment. They will at once accuse the Jews of killing our Lord, and will announce that Jesus Christ will soon be King over all the earth, and reign from Jerusalem. The Lord Himself describes these two witnesses: "These are the two olive trees and the two lampstands which stand before the Lord of the earth" (Revelation 11:4).

It follows, therefore, that they will be men of no mean repute, and this may suggest that they will be servants of God from the old economy, raised up, or raised up again for this special purpose, such as Moses and Elijah, who were previously seen on the mount of transfiguration. Or perhaps they will be Enoch and Elijah, both of whom never saw death. In any case, they will possess supernatural powers, not for their own protection, however, for the man of sin will appear and they will be treacherously slain in Jerusalem. All the world (probably through the medium of television) will see their bodies in the streets, and will rejoice at their destruction, sending presents to one another to celebrate the victory over them. It will be a short-lived pleasure that they will enjoy, for God will intervene once more to raise these two witnesses from the dead by His own direct power, and the world will see them ascend to God and to Heaven at His command.

A great earthquake will immediately follow the happenings around these two witnesses and Jerusalem itself will be seriously affected by it. Indeed, one-tenth of the city will fall to the ground, seven thousand of its people will lose their lives, and of course the remainder will become terror-stricken by the evident power of God revealed in these judgments.

Greater Abomination in Jerusalem's Temple

"He [the man of sin] takes his seat in the temple of God" (2 Thessalonians 2:4). This is much more of an abomination to God and to the people of God than that which happened in the Temple of old when Antiochus Epiphanes plundered, desecrated, and destroyed it, in B.C. 169. The Lord Jesus spoke of this as still being in the future (Matthew 24:15), which means this abomination as explained by Daniel the prophet (Daniel 9:27) cannot possibly have its complete fulfillment in the acts of Antiochus Epiphanes. In fact, it is still future, and the rage of that ancient king against the Jews and their Temple is a slight abomination in comparison to the brazen, presumptuous arrogance and devilish blasphemy of this son of perdition and his religious associate. Their wickedness against God, against the Jews, and against the new temple, which is to be built in or near Jerusalem, will be incomparable.

An image of the man of sin will be erected in the temple, and the false prophet will try to make all Jews bow before it. Many of the orthodox will refuse to worship the beast and his image. This then will soon spell the end of the covenant, and will mean the beginning of the great tribulation, the last half of the seven-year period. The fury of the forces of the man of sin will be unleashed against the Jews in Jerusalem, and the city will be in great danger of destruction or of being overrun once more by Gentile powers, or both. This covenant and its untimely breaking is spoken of by Isaiah as a covenant with death and hell, and he affirmed that it would not stand: "Hear the word of the LORD, ye . . . that rule this people . . . in Jerusalem. Because ye have said, We . . . made a covenant with death, and with hell. . . . Your covenant with death shall be disannulled, and your agreement with hell shall not stand; when the overflowing scourge [will] pass through, then ye shall be trodden down by it" (Isaiah 28:14,15,18).

The Order and Description of the Judgments

In Revelation 6–18 the details are explicit concerning the judgments in the tribulation period. There is no mention of the Church in all this section dealing with the judgment of God being poured out upon the earth, because, as the apostle puts it, unlike them "we are not [the children] of night nor of darkness. . . . For God has not destined us for wrath, but for obtaining salvation through our Lord Jesus Christ" (1 Thessalonians 5:9). The wrath he is speaking of in this context is that of the tribulation time and of the great and terrible Day of the Lord.

When John sees the first seal opened by the Lamb, the first judgment upon the earth is about to fall. Seven seals evidently enclose the scrolls containing the divine plans for this dreadful, yet righteous judgment. The first reveals a white horse and its rider. This cannot refer to Christ, because this rider brings one disaster after another. It is not the Antichrist but the man of sin, who will go forth conquering triumphantly. His haughty blasphemy will be balanced by his military power, and soon the whole world will be virtually at his feet. The second opened seal reveals a red horse wih a rider being given power to take peace from the earth. He creates political strife and civil war, the kind of warlike infiltrations we see around the world today, only on a greater scale. The pair of balances in the hand of the rider on the next horse, after the third seal is broken, speak of famine and rationing and many grievous results of worldwide inflation.

A sickly pale horse is revealed at the opening of the fourth seal. The horseman himself is named Death, followed by Hades, which, by the way, means that death is not the end, as many would like to believe! Men and beasts will be killed by his power, and one-fourth of the earth will be in ruins. The opening of the fifth seal is different. Martyrs are seen and heard, for from under the altar they cry out for vengeance by a holy God to those on earth who have slaughtered God's servants. The hour of vengeance for our God is coming soon and they are bidden to rest a little while longer before their prayer is answered. Habakkuk was given a similar answer concerning judgment on the wicked Chaldeans, when the Lord said to him, "Though it tarry, wait for it, [for] it will surely come" (Habakkuk 2:3). So also the great men and the rich see in the vision the day of God's wrath coming when seal number six is opened: "There was a great earthquake; and the sun became black as sackcloth made of hair, and the whole moon became like blood . . . stars of the sky fell to the earth . . . every mountain and island were moved out of their places. . . . The kings of the earth and the great men . . . every slave and [every] free man, hid themselves in the caves and among the rocks of the mountains . . . from the wrath of the Lamb" (Revelation 6:12-17).

The opening of the seventh seal produces an eloquent silence in Heaven. John (and we presume everyone else in Heaven) is amazed at the sight and becomes speechless. Seven angels, each with a trumpet, stand in the presence of God, about to declare a series of seven more judgments. Adoration is the only true response to the grace of God in Christ, and silence is the only possible response to the strange yet righteous judgments of God to the unrepentant. The inhabitants of Jerusalem will quake with fear as they await the storm of judgment which will follow the calm of the silence.

Seven Trumpets Sounded

The sounding by the angel of the first trumpet brings hail and fire mingled with blood to the earth. A third of the trees are burned up and so is all the grass. In our terminology it sounds like nuclear warfare! The second angel sounds his trumpet; something like a great burning mountain is cast into the sea, and a third part of the sea becomes blood. Ships and fish are destroyed. Something like a meteor has fallen on the earth!

A star falls from Heaven when the third trumpet sounds, and its name is "Wormwood." It brings bitterness to the waters, as at Marah many years before, but this time there is no salvation through a tree shown to Moses, nor through a cross given to Christ, for the day of grace is over and gone. Signs in the sun and moon and stars, as the Saviour predicted, follow the next trumpet blast. The powers of Heaven and the planets in space are shaken, and fear grips mankind. A day is coming when not only Jews in Jerusalem but all the people of the earth will look upward and begin to tremble and stagger like drunken men at the signs which will appear in the skies. Following the sounding of the fifth trumpet, men earnestly seek death, but it eludes them. For five months torment comes upon them, for the bottomless pit is opened, with smoke and darkness and agony like that from scorpion bites.

The sixth trumpet sound seems to coincide with the approach of the king of the east with an army of two hundred million, which will converge on Palestine, making for Jerusalem. China has boasted recently that this is exactly the number she can put into warfare, and it seems her approach would be through the area of the river Euphrates. Elsewhere we read of a way being made for this army, by the drying up of that very river (Revelation 16:12). A third part of men generally are slain through the conflagration which follows, but there is no sign of any repentance by those that remain, for they continue worshiping demons and idols, committing murder, taking drugs and becoming involved in immorality and theft.

The sound of the seventh trumpet reveals that God's purposes of judgment will soon be over. There is another revelation of Christ as the Mighty Angel here, setting one foot on the sea and the other on the earth, showing His authority not only over time but over the earth and all therein.

A declaration is made that Jerusalem will be trodden down of the Gentiles once more, for forty-two months, and that two of His prophets will become His witnesses in the streets of the city during this time. A real fanfare with heavenly voices proclaims Christ as the Conqueror and rightful King with all the kingdoms of the world becoming His kingdom, and all the earth filled with His glory. Shortly after these judgments are concluded Christ will appear to fulfill this prophecy.

Seven Bowls Poured Out

Seven seals broken and seven trumpets sounded, and finally seven bowls of divine wrath are poured out on the earth. Those who willingly receive the mark of the beast and worship him will unwillingly receive foul and cruel sores from the first bowl of judgment. The devil's mark of his man of sin in the foreheads of the deceived will quickly turn to the judgment mark of God.

As the second bowl is poured out the sea again becomes as blood. We have seen the results of a bloodred tide on the gulf coast of Florida, with masses of dead and stinking fish on the shore, but the pollution which is a judgment of God universally, and not simply an act of God locally, must be beyond description.

Similarly, as a result of the third outpouring, the rivers and fountains of earth become blood. In the midst of these judgments this kind of cry is heard: "O Sovereign Lord, holy and true, avenge our blood," or this one interspersed here: "Just art Thou in these Thy judgments, O Holy One." Further signs in the sun are given; men are scorched by fierce heat as the result of the fourth outpouring, and men curse their Maker.

The fifth bowl is poured out on the throne of the beast, in all probability the second beast of Revelation 13, the religious leader in Jerusalem. He is seen here enthroned in the city of the world's religious system, but he is a usurper and directs the worship of men to the man of sin, rather than to the Man of salvation. The whole of the kingdom of this beast, energized by Satan, is enshrouded in complete darkness, an added burden to the pains and sores already received. The judgments here are apparently accumulative and there is no relief.

It is when the sixth bowl is poured out that the way is prepared for the bitter and cruel king of the east to approach Palestine and the city of Jerusalem. The river Euphrates is dried up by the power of God, to make an easy and practicable crossing for the army. Evil spirits, that is, the devil's demons (there is only one devil but many demons) perform signs on earth and gather together the armies of the world to the Middle East for the great day of God Almighty, the battle of Armageddon. God will use evil men and evil powers to perform His divine purposes, as again we notice here. The Euphrates will become the eastern boundary of the land given by God to Abraham in His covenant with him. When once Gentile powers are cleared from Jerusalem, the nation of Israel will extend her borders to the river Euphrates in the east and to the river of Egypt in the southwest, the easternmost wadi of the Nile Delta.

Judgment is Finished, Jerusalem is Free

"It is done" (Revelation 16:17), a great voice cries from the new temple in Jerusalem, when the seventh bowl is emptied into the air by the angel. This prophecy portrays lightning, thunder, and an earthquake of vast proportions. Rome (called, in a spiritual sense, the great city Babylon) is split into three parts; other great cities are broken up, and some islands disappear. This earthquake may well coincide with the cleavage of the Mount of Olives, predicted for the time when Christ will appear in great power and glory. "It is done," the voice cries. The judgment is finished, the Jews are soon to be delivered, and Jerusalem will be free.

> Oh that the Lord's salvation were out of Zion come,
> To heal this ancient nation, to lead His people home.
> How long the holy city shall heathen feet profane?
> Return O Lord in pity, rebuild her walls again.

—Selected

10

JERUSALEM BESIEGED AND DELIVERED

There are some outstanding prophetical themes, stated in the clearest terms, concerning the future of Jerusalem; all nations will be gathered together against it, and the Lord Himself will eventually fight against them. Jerusalem will become a real problem to those who besiege it, "a cup of trembling" to them. As a beautiful rose has many thorns around it, so this attractive prize will present many problems to those attempting to take it.

A consecutive reading of Daniel 11 reveals something like the following order in the conflict. The king of the north (which has always been Syria), in all probability backed by Russia, as described in Ezekiel 38—39, will overrun the south and most of Palestine. The ships of the western powers (the ten-kingdom confederacy of nations) will sail against him and he will be forced to retreat. On doing so he will vent his fury against the Jews in Palestine, besiege the city of Jerusalem, and so stop the sacrifices being offered.

Those who will be dwelling in Jerusalem, under the rule of the false prophet, will replace that which will be destroyed in the temple, and restore that desecrated by the abomination of desolation. This religious leader will cause Jews to forsake the holy covenant of old, but there are some who will stand firm to Judaistic orthodoxy and even fight back. Others will fall victim to the sword or to captivity. Later on the king of the north (probably another ruler from the same area) will push south again to attack Israel, but she, together with the Arab nations around the southeast of the land, will survive his attacks. He will then proceed towards Egypt, but while there rumors concerning trouble in the north and possible attacks from the east will cause him to commence a withdrawal. On this planned return to his own land he will set up his field headquarters between Jerusalem and the Mediterranean Sea. This move by the king of the north against Israel will not only bring the western powers to intervene, but together they will by their action encourage the king of the east to do so, too. Egypt will get support from her neighbors to the south and west and will push in the same direction. The man of sin, who will be the political ruler of the ten kingdoms, will take on the role of defender of Israel and so make for the same area. "I will gather all the nations against Jerusalem to battle" (Zechariah 14:2-3).

When the Russian and Syrian armies besiege Jerusalem the first time, perhaps in the middle of the seven-year period (see Ezekiel 38:18-23), God will intervene by a great shaking, by turning each man's sword against his brother, by pestilence, and by sending lightning and great hail stones. Only one-sixth of the invading northern army will survive, the remainder will be turned back. Perhaps nuclear power, but more likely God's power, will bring them to utter defeat (Ezekiel 39:2 KJV).

Armageddon

The final intervention of God will be at the end of the tribulation time, when the other nations will converge upon the land and surround an area north of Jerusalem.

The purpose of this strategy will be not only to oppose the Jews, but it will also be an array of Gentile nations opposing one another. Roughly fifty miles directly north of Jerusalem is the wide open plain of Jezreel, near the mountain of Megiddo (the literal meaning of Armageddon).

No doubt this will become the focal point, but a far greater area around will be occupied by these forces and be overrun in the struggle. Jerusalem and even Edom further south and east will be included in the conflagration, for He, whose bloodstained garments will become red with the execution of God's wrath against His enemies, will be seen coming from Edom.

Jerusalem will be taken following its final siege, but many of the inhabitants will have fled into the wilderness, like a woman fleeing from a burning home, and will not return until Jerusalem is delivered and the King returns to reign. "Into the wilderness . . . she had a place prepared by God, so that there she might be nourished" (Revelation 12:6).

So God will send His Son and with Him ten thousands of His saints and a great army from Heaven. But it will be by the word of His mouth, His two-edged sword, that He will ignominiously defeat these armies converging on Jerusalem, and at the same time deliver His ancient people. Daniel, Zechariah, Paul, and Jude* all by the same Spirit affirm such a victory at His coming in glory and power. In fact, if it were not for His intervention at that time, with the shortening of the days of judgment, all nations of the earth would be wiped out completely by their own destructive power.

* Daniel 7:13; Zechariah 14:5; 1 Thessalonians 1:7-10; Jude 14.

One like the Son of Man will come in the clouds of Heaven, and His feet shall stand upon the Mount of Olives. That will be the first time that the Jews living then will get a glimpse of their true Messiah. His outstretched hand of power will declare Him to be the mighty Son of God. His hands, with the marks of the cross but now wielding almighty power, will show that He is the Man of Calvary, and His words will at once reveal that He is the one-time rejected King; "And one shall say unto Him, What are these wounds in Thine hands? Then He shall answer, Those with which I was wounded in the house of My friends. Awake, O sword, against My shepherd, against the man that is My fellow, saith the LORD of hosts: smite the shepherd" (Zechariah 13:6-7 KJV).

Now there are those who suggest that this is not prophetic and has nothing to do with Christ, but concerns the prophet himself or some other person. But how can that be? There is only One Person who is the fellow of the Lord of hosts, and that is the Eternal Son, and it certainly must be prophetic in character as nothing like this appearance has ever been recorded in history.

At that moment of deliverance, therefore, with such a manifestation of His mighty power, He will speak of His condescension and wounding in weakness.

> By weakness and defeat
> He won the victor's crown;
> Trod all His foes beneath His feet, By being
> trodden down.
> *Little Flock* Hymnal

*Fleeing from Jerusalem and Olivet
in the Day of the Lord*

He will immediately show that His foes were really defeated at Calvary, for at this time He will seal their doom, and Satan with his emissaries will be bound and godless nations judged.

At this appearance of Christ in power He will remind those whom He has delivered that He was wounded once in His hands; nailed through His hands to a cross of shame. "He took him by the hand and lifted him up." "He laid His hand upon him." "He . . . touched him, and said . . . I will, be thou clean," and they wounded Him in His hands!

He will remind them also that they did it; they wounded Him. "I was wounded in the house of My friends," He says in this prophetic Scripture. Little wonder that they will mourn and weep and lament and repent (as Zechariah 12:10 describes), when they are reminded so forcibly of their past rejection of the One who now in matchless grace becomes their complete Deliverer. Only a short time before this will they come to realize with all their heart that they have arrived at the end of the road. They will flee from Jerusalem into the wilderness to await their final doom. Then suddenly, their chaos is turned to peace, their distress is turned to delight, their city is swept clean of all Gentile dominion and the powers besieging it. One Man has done it all for them, and He is the God-Man, the Messiah, the once-rejected Jesus of Nazareth. A fountain shall be opened by God for their cleansing following their contrition, and "all Israel will be saved" (Romans 11:26), that is, of course, the remnant that will remain till that day.

It is also at this appearing that He will remind them that He was wounded as God's Shepherd. He had become the good Shepherd to seek the lost sheep of the house of

Israel at first, and just as a shepherd suffers wounds in his feet and hands when persistently traversing the thorny places and perilously descending the rocky slopes, so He had suffered the Just for the unjust to bring them to God. Indeed, it was to bring us all who would believe into His fold. "Although you wounded Me in My hands, when I came to you previously," He seems to say to them, "I want you to understand that God allowed it, and in a certain way Jehovah really did it." "The LORD was pleased to crush Him, putting Him to grief" (Isaiah 53:10). Zechariah also prophesied a similar revelation: "Awake, O sword, against the man that is My fellow, saith the Lord of Hosts."

It would not be surprising if in that day He would explain the reason for this incomprehensible and mysterious act of Jehovah in the words He once used while talking with Nicodemus: "For God so loved the world, He gave His unique Son" (John 3:16 margin).

Following the defeat of their enemies by the stretching forth of His wounded hands, the times of the Gentiles will be fulfilled, and the nations of earth will appear in this same period before the Lord at the judgment of the nations. Gentile world empires will be no more, their affliction of the Jews will end, and Jerusalem will be trodden under foot of the Gentiles no more forever.

11

JERUSALEM AND HER RIGHTFUL KING

At the coronation of kings of England, the archbish-op in office addresses the peers of the realm, gathered in Westminster Abbey, with these words: "Sirs, I present to you your rightful king, are you ready to pay him homage?" Upon receiving a reply in the affirmative, he moves slowly forward to place the crown on the head of the king, and every one present cries, "God save the king, God save the king, God save the king!" Jesus of Nazareth, declared to be the Son of God with power by His resur-rection from the dead, will one of these days receive the kingdom of earth from God His Father, and will wear the crown, hold the scepter, and rule from shore to shore.

It must be the most tremendous prospect for any nation or city to have the King of Glory reign as King over all the earth from it. This prospect will be realized by Jerusalem in Palestine, for in Psalm 24, the psalm of His reign, David says:

> The earth is the LORD's and all it contains,
> The world, and those [that] dwell in it. . . .
> Lift up your heads, O gates, And lift them up,
> O ancient doors, That the King of glory may come in!

Jesus Christ was "born to be King," the wise men from the east stated at His birth. But He became the re-jected King. "We will not have this man to reign over us," said the people of His day; and over His head, on the cross, His accusation was written: "This is Jesus the King of the Jews."

Following His death and resurrection, He ascended on high and the gates of glory opened wide for Him. The Father's delight with the Son's redemptive work was revealed in that to Him was given all authority and riches and wisdom and strength and honor and glory and blessing (see Revelation 5:12). Although He is reigning now in Heaven, and it is His right also to reign on earth, it is not His time, as yet, to do so, except in the hearts and lives of His own, who avow: "King of my life I crown Thee now, Thine shall the glory be." He must reign over this earth until all His enemies are overcome, hence the King of Glory will have dominion from the river to the ends of the earth. This river must be the one that shall flow in that day from the new temple, according to Ezekiel's prophecy, for there is no river at present near Jerusalem. The river Jordan is, at the nearest point, some twenty miles away.

David speaks by the Spirit and by faith as though it is a *fait accompli*: "Yet have I set My king upon My holy hill of Zion." The context of Psalm 2 shows that He was speaking of God's King, God's Son. The Prophet Isaiah (24:23) describes how "the LORD of hosts will reign on Mount Zion and in Jerusalem, and His glory will be before His elders." Isaiah prophesied, "A child will be born to us, a son will be given to us; And the government will rest on His shoulders" (Isaiah 9:6), no doubt referring to the insignia of office usually worn on the shoulder. World government as a whole will then pass to Him, whose right it is. Zechariah 14:9 takes up the same theme: "The LORD will be king over all the earth; in that day the LORD will be the only one, and His name the only one." When Ezekiel says (37:24), "My servant David will be king over them, and they will all have one shepherd," and when the throne of David is referred to in prophetic Scripture, it cannot mean the King David of old will be raised to reign from his ancient throne, but that great David's greater Son will reign over the same people as David, in the same land, and from the same city as King David of old. Peter, in his pentecostal sermon in Acts 2, asserted that David was a prophet and in that capacity said that God would raise up Christ to sit on his throne. This Jesus has God raised up, Peter asserted (see Acts 2:24), but significantly omitted the second part of David's prophecy, for He is yet to sit on His throne as King over all the earth.

His reign will be great and glorious as David proclaims: "Great is the LORD . . . in the city of our God . . . the city of the great King" (Psalm 48:1-2). His rule will be strong in righteousness and His enemies will lick the dust. "The LORD will [send] forth Thy strong scepter from Zion, saying, Rule in the midst of Thine enemies. Thy people will volunteer freely in the day of Thy power" (Psalm 110:2-3). It is God's purpose to vindicate His beloved Son completely and to make everything and everybody subordinate to Him in that day. He will be supreme as Sovereign Lord. The One who had "no beauty that we should desire Him" (Isaiah 53:2 KJV) will then become "the desire of all nations" (Haggai 2:7 margin).

At first, the reign of Christ will be for one thousand years, the meaning of millennium. This fixed period will be the vestibule of the eternal reign, for His kingdom will never be destroyed, it shall stand forever. The term "one thousand years" is used six times over of this period. It cannot be symbolic. It is a definite length of time: "The rest of the dead did not come to life until the thousand years were completed" (Revelation 20:5). If the first resurrection is literal, then the second resurrection must be literal too, as also its timing.

The Old Testament sabbath rest is a type of the millennium yet to be, and the early church fathers expressed man's time on earth in this way: 2,000 years without law, 2,000 years under law, 2,000 years under grace, 1,000 years of sabbath rest. The idea is a scriptural one (although perhaps somewhat flexible), for Peter the apostle says: "With the Lord one day is as a thousand years, and a thousand years as one day" (2 Peter 3:8).

Christians are said to be "in Christ"; they are seen by a Holy God as joined to Jesus, sharing His holiness. The moment a sinner puts his faith in the Saviour, the Holy Spirit joins him eternally in a present and complete union to his Lord. When Christ reigns over the earth, however, the Holy Spirit will do another work. It is "His kind intention which He purposed in Him with a view to an administration suitable to the fulness of times, that is, the summing up of all things in Christ" (Ephesians 1:9-10). This refers to the reign of Christ over the earth from the New Jerusalem and on the earth from the old city. David says about that day and that administration, "Men shall be blessed in Him" (Psalm 72:17 KJV). Today believers are blessed with all spiritual blessings by virtue of their union with Him, but in that day all who survive to be in His reign will, by virtue of that, share in its blessing. The scene on the mount of transfiguration, when Peter significantly said, "It is good for us to be here" (Luke 9:33), was a preview of this kingdom glory of Christ. There will be a vindication of God and of Christ and of His Church,

too, before the history of this present earth closes, for
the nations will participate (some more than others) in
the reign of our Lord, and He is the One they will honor.
"He will not . . .[fail] until He has established justice
in the earth" (Isaiah 42:4). That has not yet happened,
but He cannot fail, for He is God.

Nature will be redeemed from the curse when Jesus
reigns. There will be a marked increase in the fruitfulness
of the ground. Corn will grow in abundance, even on top
of mountains (Psalm 72:16), and many things impossible
today will become a reality. The wolf will dwell with the
lamb, the lion will eat straw like a bullock, and nothing
will hurt or destroy.

The sun, as usual, will rise and fall over the old city,
a contrast to the New Jerusalem, with no need for the sun,
"the Lamb is the light." When the Sun of Righteousness
arises with healing in His wings (Malachi 4:2), the whole
earth will at last be filled with the knowledge of God and
will rise to receive the blessing of its Redeemer.

Jerusalem will never be able to live up to her name,
"the habitation of peace," until the Prince of Peace is
acclaimed as her ruler. There will be no fear of the nations
around when justice reigns. In the Messianic psalms, David
speaks of the God-Man reigning as King over the entire
earth: "Thy throne, O God, is forever and ever; A scepter
of uprightness is the scepter of Thy kingdom. Thou hast
loved righteousness" (Psalm 45:6). Again he affirms, "In
His days may the righteous flourish, And abundance of
peace till the moon is no more" (Psalm 72:7). Things will
work together for good for those in Jerusalem and for
all who will enjoy participating in His reign: "The work
of righteousness will be peace, And the service of righteousness, quietness and confidence forever. Then My

people will live in a peaceable habitation, And in secure dwellings and in undisturbed resting places" (Isaiah 32:17-18). Then there will be no more war, and Jerusalem will never face destruction again, for "He shall judge between the nations . . . they [shall] hammer their swords into plowshares, and their spears into pruning hooks. Nation [shall] not lift up sword against nation, And never again will they learn war" (Isaiah 2:4).

Misery Excluded in His Reign

No minority misery will disrupt the city then: "With righteousness He will judge the poor, And decide with fairness for the afflicted of the earth . . . faithfulness [will be] the belt about His waist" (Isaiah 11:4-5). "I will make peace your administrators, And righteousness your overseers. Violence will not be heard again in your land, Nor devastation or destruction within your borders; But you will call your walls salvation, and your gates praise" (Isaiah 60:17-18). So will end the political policies and perilous pacts of a godless society; man's methods of personal power seeking will come to an end when God the Father hands over to His Son all authority on earth, as He now possesses authority in Heaven. The extreme contrast between the sorrows of Jerusalem in days gone by, and the joys to be experienced by the people in His reign are striking, to say the least. "You will have the LORD for an everlasting light, And the days of your mourning will be finished. Then all your people will be righteous; They will possess the land forever" (Isaiah 60:20-21).

There is an outward form of prosperity in Jerusalem today, but within there is poverty and discontent. With such a large percentage of the gross national product being spent on arms, for fear of their enemies around, such a small state as Israel could not become truly prosperous, but in the thousand-year reign of our Lord "they shall no more be a prey to the nations, they shall dwell safely, the earth shall yield her increase, there shall be showers of blessing" (Ezekiel 34:26-28 KJV). "In this mountain shall the LORD of hosts make . . . all people a feast of fat things. . . . He will swallow up death in victory" (Isaiah 25:6,8 KJV). The land of Palestine will be fruitful, the ground shall yield her increase, and the remnant of this people shall possess all these things. "You were a curse, so I will save you that you may become a blessing. Do not fear" (Zechariah 8:13).

The plain statement of prophecy is really filled with significant import: "Then it will come about that any who are left of all the nations that went up against Jerusalem will go up from year to year to worship the King" (Zechariah 14:16). When the judgment of Israel is finished, when the Lord Jesus has appeared as the Fellow of the Lord of Hosts and the mighty Conqueror, when the enemies of Jerusalem are overcome, the city is free, and the Christ of the cross has become the King, reigning over all the earth, then worship will commence. The One who was rejected will be owned as Deliverer, Saviour, and Messiah; He who was cast out and slain will be on the throne, the object of true worship. He will be honored by all the nations in the very city where He was accused and set at nought. Then Jerusalem will be the center for the worship of God, not only for the Jewish race, but for all the nations of the earth.

Just as the heavenly Jerusalem above will never come down to earth, so the earthly Jerusalem will never leave the earth, but it will surely be extended and made more glorious, suitable to be the center of our Lord's earthly reign. Representatives of countries around the world will honor the One on the throne, and bring treasures from their lands to Jerusalem, not so much to glorify the city as to exalt the King.

Jerusalem will be the seat of government in the age to come. The laws of the King of kings will go forth from it, making her a praise among the nations, for the laws will be righteous, for the general good and spiritual blessing of men. Today, unfortunately, old Jerusalem is the center of conflict and trouble, but then, in His day, she will be the joy of all the earth.

Jerusalem the Holy City Again

"The temple of God" is the descriptive metaphor given by the Apostle Paul to describe the believer's body, undoubtedly because the Holy Spirit of God dwells there. Similarly Jerusalem will become in reality the holy city of the earth, because the throne of our holy Lord will be within its gates. This indeed was the divine intention, why Jehovah was pleased to place His name there, and make His presence known in the sanctuary within her. Nothing short of divine holiness will be the standard of this holy city. Even the houses and their furniture will be consecrated to God, the pots in which the food will be cooked, and the common domestic utensils will be stamped with the insignia: "HOLY TO THE LORD" (see Zechariah 14:20).

The Prophet Zechariah also adds that the bridles of the horses with their bells and trappings will, in that day, sound forth the holiness of the King. "He who is left in

Zion and remains in Jerusalem will be called holy . . .
everyone who is recorded for life in Jerusalem. When
the LORD has washed away the filth of the daughters of
Zion, and [has] purged the bloodshed of Jerusalem from
her midst, by the spirit of judgment and the spirit of
burning" (Isaiah 4:3-4).

The righteous reign of Christ from Jerusalem will
not, however, appeal to all of mankind during the millennium. There will still be unregenerate people with fall-
en human natures, unchanged and unrepentant, who will
wish to be as far away as possible from the holiness and
righteousness of Christ. "The whole earth will be filled
with His glory," we read, which means there will be manifestation of the divine attributes of the King throughout
the entire world, but some will want to get away from
that kind of spiritual influence, and thus will gravitate
and migrate to the four corners of the earth (Revelation
20:7-10). These people and their many descendants will
become the Gog and Magog named in Revelation 20 (but
they are not identical with the Gog of Ezekiel 38–39
who invade Palestine before the millennium commences).
Fredk. A. Tatford says, "The Gog of Ezekiel is a proto-
type of the apocalyptic people of Gog."

In the wisdom of God, Satan will be released after
being bound for one thousand years and will immediately
recommence his opposition to holiness and to Christ.
Moving people to revolt, he will lead an assault on the city
of Jerusalem. Why will God release Satan when there is
equity and peace and prosperity in the earth? Perhaps He
will wish to demonstrate finally that the heart of unregenerate man has an incurable bias to evil and is still in
constant rebellion against Himself; or maybe He intends
to declare that not even a reign in righteousness with a

rod of iron will transform the nature of fallen men, which can be accomplished only by divine grace through the indwelling of the Spirit of Jesus Christ; or perhaps both.

Jerusalem Finally Protected

There will be a final vain attempt to overthrow God's King, with Jerusalem the center of this rebellion. The Jews with their authority and the city of Jerusalem with its glory will become an acrimonious pill for the rebels to swallow. Satan will cause them to resent their forced submission to the Jewish rulers, bringing them to Jerusalem to besiege it. Maybe it will happen almost unnoticed at the time of the feast of tabernacles, with the crowds in and around the capital, coming to honor the King, as they will be required to do annually. There will be no visible revelation of the King in power and glory, no divine sword to intervene, no armies of Jews put on alert. But before an assault is actually put into operation, God Himself will send fire from Heaven and they will be consumed in a moment, and the subjugation of rebellious men, together with the devil who has deceived them, will be complete.

Satan commenced his downward fall when he was still in Heaven; lawlessness filled his heart and he was brought down in disgrace from the mountain of God (see Ezekiel 28:15-16). Our Lord not only explained that this was the reason for Satan's fall, but that He actually saw it: "I was watching Satan fall from heaven like lightning" (Luke 10:18). Then, according to Revelation 12, he will fall again from his realm in the first heaven, when he will be cast out by Michael the archangel, and will come to earth in person (not bodily). He will be bound in the abyss (Revelation 20:3), and that will mean a further fall to last for a thousand years. But finally his downward path will end when he will be cast into the lake of fire forever.

Jerusalem then will be free, Palestine will enjoy the divine benevolence, and the earth will be filled with the glory of its King. Nevertheless the holiness of God will call for a new Heaven and new earth where no taint of sin has ever come. Only thus will the Father vindicate His Son and fulfill His holy purpose. "The heavens will pass away with a roar and the elements will be destroyed with intense heat, and the earth and its works will be burned up. . . . But according to His promise we are looking for new heavens and a new earth, in which righteousness dwells" (2 Peter 3:10,13).

It goes without saying that it is the first heaven, the atmospheric heaven around the earth, which is in question here. The Heaven which is the dwelling place of God certainly will not be burned up. As we have shown earlier, this is to be the place of the New Jerusalem before she comes out of this third Heaven from God again, the second time, to enjoy the eternal state when God will be all in all.

12

OLD JERUSALEM AND THE NEW TEMPLE

Jerusalem has been what it has been because of the Temple within her walls, the one dwelling place on earth of Jehovah. The city and the Temple cannot be divorced, and even today the city is sacred to the Jews, not only because of its historical associations with their ancestors but because of the west wall of the temple of Herod, which still remains, known as the wailing wall.

The rebuilding of the temple may well be the greatest desire of hundreds of thousands of Jews, for Jerusalem can become the most glorious city again only as the glorious temple is once more rebuilt. Herod's temple covered a square of approximately one thousand feet; in contrast, St. Paul's cathedral in London is five hundred twenty feet long. The temple as seen by Ezekiel is five times longer than that of Herod, and ten times the size of St. Paul's. It is inside this newly constructed temple that the abomination of desolation will be set up during the second half of Daniel's seventieth week, the tribulation period. This was confirmed by our Lord in the Gospels as something to be fulfilled in the future; therefore it could not possibly have had its fulfillment in B.C. 169, when Antiochus Epiphanes sacrificed a pig on the altar. The abomination which makes desolate is to be an image of the first beast as seen in Revelation 13, the man of sin, the political head of the ten-kingdom confederacy, pictured in the ten toes of Nebuchadnezzar's image. It is the second beast in Revelation 13 who is the religious head, the Antichrist, who causes the people of that day to worship the image of the man of sin in the temple.

Other Views of the Prophecy

It is understandable why some students of prophecy are inclined to ignore altogether Ezekiel's message concerning the temple and the sacrifices. Others dismiss it as a vision which the prophet had, without any special significance. Some believe it is meant to be a type only of a certain aspect of church truth. The problem which looms largest in the minds of these Bible teachers concerns the reintroduction of bloody sacrifices. "For what purpose is all this?" they ask, "and how dangerous to belittle the all-sufficient and once-for-all sacrifice of Christ on the cross!"

First of all, then let us consider this latter point, especially from Hebrews 9:12, where the writer says concerning Christ: "Who does not need daily . . . to offer up sacrifices . . . because this He did once for all when He offered up Himself" (Hebrews 7:27). "He entered [into] the holy place once for all, having obtained eternal redemption. . . . Once at the consummation He has been manifested to put away sin by the sacrifice of Himself."

It must be stated categorically that the Scriptures teach there is to be no more offering for sin, because Christ's offering was sufficient for all people and for all time and therefore was "once for all." Ezekiel, however, was a prophet of God and the prophecies contained in the last eight chapters of His book have not yet been fulfilled. Because He spoke as one inspired by the Holy Spirit, we must expect a fulfillment in the future.

Ezekiel's introduction to his last eight chapters about the temple and its sacrifices is most significant, where God speaks: "Now I shall restore the fortunes of Jacob, and have mercy on the whole house of Israel. . . . And they shall forget their disgrace. . . . When I bring them back . . . and gather them from the lands of their enemies, then I shall be sanctified through them in the [midst] of the many nations . . . and [I] gathered them again to their own land. . . . And I will not hide My face from them any longer, for I shall have poured out My Spirit on the house of Israel" (Ezekiel 39:25-29).

Isaiah, Daniel, Jeremiah, Zechariah, and the Apostle John corroborate that which was given in detail to Ezekiel. For instance, Isaiah 56:7 says, "Even those I will bring to My holy mountain, And make them joyful in My house of prayer. Their burnt offerings and their sacrifices will be acceptable on My altar; For My house will be called a house of prayer for all the peoples."

The Regathering of Israel Calls for a New Temple

The context of this passage concerns the time when the outcasts of Israel will be regathered. "They shall bring all your brethren for an offering unto the LORD [from] out of all nations . . . to My holy mountain . . . saith the LORD, as the children of Israel bring an offering in a clean vessel into the house of the LORD. . . . All flesh shall come to worship before Me, saith the Lord" (Isaiah 66:20,23).

The temple will be rebuilt in or near Jerusalem before the millennial period commences. Can anyone, in all seriousness, imagine the Jews to be in control of the holy city of Jerusalem year after year, and to resort continually to the wailing wall, without thinking of or praying for its rebuilding? The Scripture in Ezekiel and elsewhere asserts that a literal fulfillment is essential. True, the dimensions of Ezekiel's temple would be too great for the present temple site in the old city, but then Ezekiel does not see it in that area exactly, but in the section of the land called "the holy oblation," the division reserved for the priests south of Jerusalem. This area will be fifty miles wide.

Dr. Walvoord, in his work on the millennial kingdom, says of the rebuilding of the temple: "If it was intended to be a typical presentation only, to be fulfilled by the Church in this present age, it would raise many problems and no exegesis would be possible." It is interesting, to say the least, that the most recent of the Dead Sea scrolls, the so-called temple scroll, speaks of God creating the final temple Himself.

In an article, "The Newest of the Dead Sea Scrolls," in the January 1977 *Time* magazine, is a statement that the Essenes (the Jewish sect which wrote or copied the scrolls) repudiated worship at the Herodian temple in Jerusalem because they believed it to be corrupt. It is concluded by some that the teaching of this temple scroll (the longest of the Dead Sea scrolls) is that God Himself would create the final temple "on the day of blessing . . . I will create My temple and establish it for all time." Our Lord Himself taught (Matthew 24:15) that a time would come in the future when there would be another temple erected in which would be placed the abomination that maketh desolate. Daniel spoke of this on two occasions, both of which, we are sure, Christ had in His mind when He made the above statement. First at the end of chapter 9 Daniel talks of "the overspreading of [the] abominations that make desolate," that would put a stop to the sacrifice and grain offering, and complete destruction will then be poured out upon the desolater. Again Daniel 11:31 affirms, "Forces . . . will arise, desecrate the sanctuary . . . do away with the regular sacrifice. And they will set up the abomination of desolation."

As, in the time of our Lord on earth, the fulfillment of this must have been in the future, for Him to make such a prophecy, and as history records no such happening since, we may safely conclude that it remains for future fulfillment. A new temple and sanctuary have yet to be built.

Memorial Sacrifices Only

Sacrifices are to be literally observed, but because of our Lord's once-for-all sacrifice these will be offered only as a memorial, looking back retrospectively to Christ, just as the sacrifices instituted by Moses looked forward prospectively to Christ. These in the millennial reign will be no more expiatory than were those in Moses' day. An example of this is seen in the Lord's Supper. The ordinance is literally fulfilled but it is a memorial feast, a looking back to the finished work of Christ. A memorial was never intended to be equal in effect to the real sacrifice, but it certainly points directly to the reality, which is Christ.

The words of our Lord are significant: "I shall never again eat it until it is fulfilled in the kingdom of God" (Luke 22:16). "I will not drink of the fruit of the vine from now on until that day when I drink it new with you in My Father's kingdom" (Matthew 26:29). It seems therefore that He is plainly stating that in the kingdom of God on earth, in a future day, He will participate in a feast with His own, and at that time they together would be looking back to His once-for-all sacrifice.

The feast of tabernacles, which is to be held in Jerusalem in the day of His power, may very well be this feast spoken of by our Lord, and in which He Himself will participate: "I will return to Zion and will dwell in the midst of Jerusalem" (Zechariah 8:3), and again in the same prophecy: "I will be the glory in her midst" (Zechariah 2:5). It is first in the new temple that His glory will be revealed, but Jerusalem will share in the glory, as indeed will the whole earth, which will then be covered by the glory of the Lord, as the waters cover the sea.

When the first Temple had been built by Solomon and the prayer of consecration had been said, "the glory of the LORD filled the house." History will repeat itself once more when the Redeemer shall come to Zion; "Arise, shine; for your light has come, And the glory of the LORD has risen upon you. . . . His glory will appear upon you. And the nations will come to your light, And kings to the brightness of your rising. . . . They will bring gold and frankincense, And will bear good news of the praises of the LORD. . . . I shall glorify My glorious house. . . . In My wrath I struck you, And in My favor I have had compassion on you. . . . The glory of Lebanon will come to you . . . To beautify the place of My sanctuary; And I [will] make the place of My feet glorious. . . . They will call you the city of the LORD, the Zion of the Holy One of Israel" (Isaiah 60:1-14). "And the name of the city from that day shall be [Jehovah Shammah], The LORD is there" (Ezekiel 48:35). "And the Lord . . . will suddenly come to His temple" (Malachi 3:1).

In concluding this section on the new temple, we confess that there are difficulties, in relation to its interpretation, with every school of thought. We appreciate that to some there are details here which seem improbable, and because of that will be accepted by them as symbolic only. On the other hand we believe that the fullness of detail in these last chapters of Ezekiel favors a literal interpretation. However, faith will wait on God for a fulfillment of His Word through His prophet, in His own way as well as in His own time. It should be noted, finally, that Ezekiel, in His description of the temple with its surroundings and the suburbs of the city, makes ample arrangements for universal worship, and universal worship of Christ the King is sure.

13

THE NEW JERUSALEM HERSELF

The Builder and Maker of this city is God Himself, and God does not make His cities of concrete and stone mined from the hills of earth. No, this Jerusalem is a new city, and everything concerning it is new. It is constructed of new heavenly materials, its size is new for a city, its location is new, its perfections and pleasures and permanence are new. Divine things and spiritual things are always new! God has given to His people now a new life in Christ His Son: "If any man is in Christ, he is a new creature" (2 Corinthians 5:17). It is not that Christians have some new ideas for living, but they have a new life implanted within them. At regeneration they become partakers of the divine nature, and so they are newborn babes, who belong to a new realm. Christ by His Spirit is the life of their lives, and these they live under a new covenant of grace, the consummation of which is the possession of a new name and a participation in life in the New Jerusalem. "Behold, I make all things new" (Revelation 21:5 KJV).

"A Place for You" in Heaven

The Lord Jesus Christ once said to His own: "I go to prepare a place for you" (John 14:1), and the New Jerusalem is without doubt the place He has gone to prepare. It is His going into Heaven which is the guarantee for His own that there is a place in Heaven for them, too. The entrance He made by virtue of His own shed blood is the pledge that they who trust that same redeeming blood have a place prepared for them in the New Jerusalem. The place is now in Heaven, but it will descend out of Heaven one day to be the home of the redeemed during the reign of Christ over the earth. The Apostle Paul speaks of the "New Jerusalem which is above," and that is in keeping with his teaching elsewhere, that the believer's hope and inheritance are both in Heaven. Heaven and the New Jerusalem are the home of the Christian. His future abode is not to be on earth, and the Bible shows it never will be on the earth. The Christian is described in the New Testament as a pilgrim and a stranger on this planet, or as the NEB renders it, "an alien in a foreign land." Elsewhere he is called an ambassador, which suggests that he is meant to be the representative of his King in another realm. "Our citizenship is in heaven, from which also we eagerly wait for a Saviour, the Lord Jesus Christ; who will transform the body of our humble state into conformity with the body of His glory" (Philippians 3:20-21).

The reason for this change is that the Christian might feel at home in Heaven. "We have . . . a house not made with hands, eternal in the heavens" (2 Corinthians 5:1), a contrast with the tent of the believer's body in this earthly scene. "We shall . . . bear the image of the heavenly," (1 Corinthians 15:49), the apostle also declares and in 2 Timothy 4:18 he adds this testimony, "The Lord will deliver me . . . and . . . bring me safely to His heavenly kingdom." To the Colossian Christians he speaks of "the hope laid up for you in heaven," and again, "the Father has qualified us to share in the inheritance of the saints in light" (Colossians 1:5,12), meaning the saints who are in Heaven already. Finally, as if to clear up the point that Heaven with its New Jerusalem and not the earth is the future home of the saved, Paul says, "When Christ, who is our life, is revealed, then you also will be revealed with Him in glory" (Colossians 3:4). Glorified with Him, in glorified bodies, with which to live in glory. Who then among His own would wish to dwell for a thousand years more on this weary war-torn planet earth?

Christ will bring many sons to glory, said the writer of the Epistle to the Hebrews and because this was in view he could encourage his readers to suffer joyfully the spoiling of their goods. They had in Heaven "a better and an enduring substance" (Hebrews 10:34 KJV). Another who joins in this general theme of glory in Heaven by and by is the Apostle Peter: "This way of suffering leads on to heavenly glory," and the example he uses is that of our Lord, whose path of pain and suffering has already been followed by His present session in the glory of Heaven. "It is the way the Master went, Should not the servant tread it still?" As he expands the same theme, 1 Peter 1:4 speaks of the inheritance there "reserved in heaven for you," for those who suffer with Christ now will reign with Him over the earth in the New Jerusalem in a day to come.

Abraham looked for this new city, "Whose architect and builder is God," and it is referred to as "the city of the living God" (Hebrews 11:10;12:22). From this we gather it must be a living city and a God-built city, as opposed to the old Jerusalem which is in Palestine, and all that that city stands for in Judaism. Christians not only come to the heavenly Jerusalem, through their hope in Christ, but also to an innumerable company of angels. This place has associations with the heavenly host. "You have come to the general assembly and Church of the first-born . . . and to God, the judge of all" (Hebrews 12:22-24). This is an "ekklesia," a called-out company of all believers. When they arrive in the New Jerusalem, they come "to the spirits of righteous men made perfect, and to Jesus, the mediator of a new covenant." What a beautiful city, with the Living God, Jesus, angels, and righteous men made perfect! At last the purpose of God will be fulfilled, when He Himself makes His home with man, His own creature, a purpose hindered by the fall, but then brought to complete fruition in the New Jerusalem.

The New Jerusalem is divine in both origin and character, "the . . . city [of my God, which comes] down out of heaven from God" (Revelation 21:10). John describes, with the use of many symbols, what he saw in his vision. It is true that symbols are sometimes difficult to interpret, but we must remember that the apocalypse is meant to be a revelation, as its title suggests, and not a mystification.

A Spiritual Vision

John was carried away *in the spirit* to a high mountain to view the bride, the Lamb's wife, the New Jerusalem. He was in the spirit and not in the flesh, when he was with the angel on the high mountain. The same phrase is used earlier: "I was in the spirit; and behold, a throne was [set] in heaven" (Revelation 4:2). It was an angel who carried John away (for all angels are spirits), and he was carried, not on his wings, we take it, but only in spirit to the high mountain. Because of this fact we are forced to interpret some of these descriptions as symbolic. However, this must never be allowed to give the impression that a symbol is a suggestion of something

unreal or less important than the literal thing might be. Indeed, if the symbol is seen to be so wonderful or so vast or so dazzling, then what the reality will be no tongue could ever describe.

Rather than belittling the hope of the Church, we wish to show that New Jerusalem is much more glorious than any literal exposition could ever explain it to be. It has "not entered the heart of man, all that God has prepared for those who love Him" (1 Corinthians 2:9). Human hearts can never grasp the fullness of the eternal blessings which await the redeemed. (However, Paul does say, "God revealed them through the Spirit"; for instance, here in the Revelation the Spirit reveals to us some idea, as much as we can bear now, of what God has prepared for them that love Him. Indeed, a foretaste or guarantee of the indescribable eternal glory yet to be fully revealed has already been made real to His own by the gift of the Holy Spirit and His indwelling, enjoyed by every true believer in Christ. "The Holy Spirit of promise . . . is . . . a pledge of our inheritance" [Ephesians 1:13-14].)

So John was there on the high mountain in spirit, and he saw the New Jerusalem only with the eyes of his soul, and it may be quite true to say that his physical eyes never saw the city foursquare, and his physical hands never measured a literal city about 1,500 miles in each direction. It is significant that inspiration never attempted to indicate the shape of the city, whether a cube or a pyramid or some other form. "John is concerned with spiritual states rather than physical realities," says Tasker, the British theologian. The Holy City is not a mass of concrete and

Vision of the Apostle John
On the Isle of Patmos

metal, but it consists of people who have their names in the book of life. The implications or underlying realities which are suggested by any symbols used are the important things to be understood. The size mentioned, if not literal, must mean that the city is so vast that there is room for all the saints of all ages. Tammas, the New Zealand engineer, has pointed out that the actual dimensions of this city would be 2,250,000 square miles, fifteen thousand times as big as London or twenty times as big as the whole of New Zealand. The measuring of the city with a rod, which was at the most ten feet in length, must have been to impress the apostle with the size of the heavenly home. The question may well be asked, "Whoever would undertake such a task of literally measuring, with a rod of that length only, a city 1,500 miles long and 1,500 miles wide and even struggle to measure its height, 1,500 miles into space?"

The symbol of gold used often in this description must mean that this city is more glorious—with divine glory, that is, and not with earthly gold—than we can here understand. Earthly gold is not transparent at all, however much refined, and this gold is said to be as transparent as glass. But what it is actually going to be has not yet entered into the heart of man. The sure thing is, it is to be more glorious than gold as we know it to be.

John records that the angel took him in spirit to a great high mountain to show him the bride, the Lamb's wife, and when he looked on the scene before him, behold the bride was a great city. Now this city was the Lamb's bride, not because of anything which made it a city, but because of the glorified saints who inhabited it. An actual city built by man is not a person at all; but on the other hand, a city is not a city if it is not made up of persons dwelling there. It was the people, the children of Israel, who were reckoned as the wife of Jehovah, and it is the people who comprise the Church who are reckoned as the bride of the Lamb. Therefore New Jerusalem, whatever else literally it may be, in the first place is the company of the redeemed. W.E. Vine points out in his dictionary of New Testament Greek words: "By metonymy, the word 'city' stands for the inhabitants as in Matthew 21:10, 'The [whole] city was moved, saying, Who is this?'." The people who form the bride are certainly in a place, but even that may not mean the same kind of place, as we understand the term. They are seen to be over the earth, having descended out of Heaven, the dwelling place of God, into the heaven of space, the second heaven, and they share with Christ, their heavenly Bridegroom, His kingly reign over the earth.

This real heavenly community is the company of the saved from all time periods of the past and present, and it is seen that God the Father dwells in the midst of them, that this communion is eternal, and sin is forever outside. The Apostle Paul uses symbols of the Church in the letter to the Ephesians: a body, a building, and a bride. Why should some question this concept of a city in the heavens as a most suitable symbol of the Church in the form it will assume in the future, and going right on into the eternal state?

It would be difficult to find one single expositor who claimed that everything in this last book of the Bible should be interpreted literally. Perhaps the rule here should be (as indeed elsewhere in the Scriptures), "When the actual sense makes good sense, seek no other sense." Although it is agreed there is much in the book of Revelation which should be taken quite literally (and it would be a mistake to spiritualize when it is evident from the context that the subject is spoken of in a literal way, and is meant to be understood literally), it is a book of symbols to a great extent. Almost all expositors, of whatever school of thought, insert from time to time a little symbolism in their writings on Revelation.

The harlot, or the false religion, was seen earlier in this prophecy as a city reigning over the kings of the earth. Here is the bride of the Lamb, seen similarly as a city, but in contrast as a holy city, for they who form it are a holy nation. Again this New Jerusalem is in a special relationship to the Lord Himself. Surely our Lord has no relationship to an actual city with walls, streets, metals, precious stones, rivers, and trees, but to a people He has purchased for Himself. Although it is true that the redeemed will be with their Lord in His reign over the earth, it should be remembered that they, in their glorified bodies, do not need walls to keep them in, nor gates to let them in, or literal streets of gold on which to walk. Our Lord in His glorified body (and they will have bodies like His) was not kept away from His own by closed doors and neither was He kept down by the law of gravitation. The house we have in the heavens, whose sole Architect is God, is "not made with hands." It is a heavenly and an eternal habitation, for the Eternal God is the Maker.

We also take it, therefore, that the idea of a Lamb in the city is not literal either, but symbolical of Christ as the Pascal Lamb of God's providing for the redemption of sinners, who are now saved and present with Him in the New Jerusalem. In other words, we are being reminded that His own people will always remember that they are there with Him to share His glory and His reign, all because of Calvary. "Forever as the Lamb once slain, Shall I remember Thee."

The idea of a city is a great company of saints who will be together with their Lord. The gold indicates that the glory of God is past their comprehension. The bride, the Lamb's wife and her adorning, is a confirmation that the city is holy; that Christ's own people, purchased to be His bride, are clad entirely with His own righteousness, which has been imputed to them.

Security in the New Jerusalem

The wide disproportion between the height of the city and the breadth of the walls has often been noticed, for one does not need training in architecture to understand that 72 yards (144 cubits) is not sufficient width for a wall 1,500 miles high! If it is assumed that 72 yards refers to the height of the wall, then the question arises as to why a wall is needed at all when the city is built 1,500 miles high? As God dwells within those walls and angels are at the gates, protection and security are by these walls proclaimed. The names of the twelve tribes of Israel are written on the gates of the city, again a reminder of the privileged position of Israel throughout the years, and of God's faithfulness to His covenant with them. These twelve gates are each made of a single pearl, and this too is far beyond one's imagination. But, as Matthew Henry states, "There is nothing magnificent enough in this world, fully to set forth the glory of Heaven." Does it mean that twelve tiny shellfish have each produced a huge pearl from a minute foreign substance within their shells, which they covered with a type of saliva? Was it then hardened through thousands of years to make a genuine pearl many yards in diameter through which people may enter? (We are told it takes years for an oyster to make one small pearl of one-quarter inch diameter.) No! but so beautiful is a real pearl that this jewel alone can describe for us, in terms we can comprehend, the way into the city of God.

The foundations of the walls of cities we know are very rarely seen, but here they are described as not only visible to the Apostle John, but he could also see the names of the twelve apostles of the Lamb inscribed on them. Are we to understand that John saw with his physical eyes, not only all the foundations of this vast city, and the names of the apostles in the foundations, but even those on the far side some 1,500 miles away? Or was it that the angel told him, in the vision, what was written thereon? Surely the idea means to convey that this company of the saved owe their secure spiritual foundation, in respect to their future, to the twelve apostles of our Lord (as well as to the Lamb Himself), for it was their doctrine about Jesus Christ, the One they knew so well, which enlightened their minds about His glorious person and His work on their behalf. The Church will always remember, therefore, that she is built upon the foundation of the apostles and prophets. John saw the foundation garnished with all manner of precious stones, all so colorful, bringing to our minds the colors of the rainbow—again a memorial to His faithfulness in keeping His covenant with men.

A Heavenly River and Tree of Life

The symbolic idea of the river of life denotes that in the future the Church will enjoy superabundant life and everflowing blessing from God Himself; for rivers, as we know them, never have their springs in a literal throne, but incidentally in a high mountain! As the river of life so also the tree of life (a traditional feature of paradise). Sin will not keep the saints from the tree of life in that day, as Adam and Eve were kept from Eden's tree, and this is a further emphasis that the life more abundant, which our Lord came to give, will be the portion of the saved without measure in the New Jerusalem. Continuous fruit from this tree of life speaks of the perpetual satisfying portion, with no barren seasons. The leaves of the tree, which are for the health or healing of the nations, can only be symbolical of the fact that the Church in her reign with Christ, although not on the earth, will in some particular ways bring blessing to the nations on earth. The "whole earth [will] be filled with His glory. . . . And men shall be blessed in Him" (Psalm 72:19,17), that is, in His reign. The nations of them that are saved walk in the light of God and in the light of the city of God, and they will be maintained with a healthy righteousness by the influence of the New Jerusalem.

For the sake of our peace of mind and for our own blessed assurance for the future state, we should remember that although things in this city will be far superior to anything we have seen or known on earth, and indeed far more glorious than any description we have read or heard about, it is an impossibility to describe adequately to earthly creatures of time, heavenly spiritual things of eternity. No wonder we poor humans have difficulty in understanding objects and situations in the heavenly sphere! Just imagine the difficulty one would encounter in trying to explain to an African Zulu the working of an electric refrigerator when he only knows about the cool-

ing waters of his tribal stream! So, here is the Apostle
John struggling to explain in earthly terminology a
vision he had in the spirit of the home of the Church in
Heaven and coming out of Heaven, a vision in fact given to
him by an angel. And, although it is a brave attempt that
he makes, we are sure he would be the first to admit
that the language he uses is really most inadequate to
describe what he saw.

> My Father's house on high,
> Home of my soul how near,
> At times to faith's transparent eye,
> Thy pearly gates appear!
> My thirsty spirit faints
> To reach the land I love,
> The bright inheritance of saints,
> Jerusalem above.

14

THE NEW JERUSALEM, WHERE AND WHEN

Heaven, the eternal home of the saved, is described in the New Testament in various ways in order that there may be a fuller understanding of its glories. In the Gospel of Luke it is called a country, suggesting its vastness. In Hebrews it is spoken of as a city, giving a better understanding of its inhabitants. It is named a kingdom in Second Peter assuring its orderliness. Paradise is the name given to it in Revelation, a reminder of its delight. It is also called "My Father's house" by the Son Himself in the Gospel of John, speaking of the relationships of the heavenly family.

Scripture speaks of three heavens. The first is the atmospheric heaven, made by God on the second day of creation, which will pass away with a great noise at the end of the millennium, according to Peter's prophecy, and which eventually will be replaced by a new heaven. The second Heaven declares the glory of God (Psalm 19:1), the starry heaven of space, "stretched out like a curtain" (Isaiah 40:22). The third Heaven is the dwelling place of God, "the heaven of heavens" (1 Kings 8:27). Paul the apostle was caught up to the third Heaven (2 Corinthians 12:2). Our Lord's sample prayer commences, "Our Father which art in heaven" (Luke 11:2).

The Lord Jesus is said to have passed through the heavens and into Heaven itself (Hebrews 9:24). Similarly we understand that New Jerusalem will come out of

Heaven and into the heavens (Revelation 21:2). This does not mean to suggest that she will come down to the earth. Indeed, it would be a geographical impossibility for a city of this size (1,500 miles each way) to rest on the earth in Palestine. She will remain over the earth, as man-made satellites do today, and be a small part of the Heaven of heavens, but situated at that time in the second heaven, the heaven of space; and the nations of the earth will bring their glory and honor unto it (not into it!). This positioning of the saints in the New Jerusalem over the earth will be, at first, for a period of 1,000 years. They will be in the presence of their Lord even there; "Where Jesus is 'tis heaven there."

Three separate places and time periods are suggested in Scripture for the existence and positioning of the New Jerusalem, the holy city. She is seen in Heaven, God's dwelling place, during the time of tribulation. Then she appears in space, over the earth, during the thousand years' reign of Christ. She finally comes out of Heaven from God once more, at the commencement of the eternal state, to make her presence known both in the new Heaven and the new earth. If she is seen at first coming down from God out of Heaven, it implies that she has been with God in Heaven prior to this. This must surely be during the time calculated to be Daniel's seventieth week, the time of Jacob's trouble, the tribulation. Our Lord was evidently referring to this place in Heaven when He said to His own, "Let not your heart be troubled. . . . In My Father's house are many dwelling places . . . I go to prepare a place for you" (John 14:1-2).

The Church will take part in the first resurrection, when the dead in Christ will be raised, that is, when this perishable will have put on the imperishable, and the living saints changed (see 1 Corinthians 15:54), (when mortal shall put on immortality at the rapture). She will meet the Lord in the air, and then be in His presence forever. Being caught up together with them (the loved ones in Christ gone on before) is certainly a comforting thought, but to live together with Him is indeed the most comforting. "He whom having not seen we love." We shall then see Him, and abide with Him forever, but at first in the Father's house. Following this translation of the Church, she will be taken to dwell in Heaven with Christ, and that must be the New Jerusalem, the place He has gone to prepare.

The Two Stages of His Coming

It is very much in evidence in the Scriptures that the second coming of the Lord Jesus will be staged in the following precise way for two reasons. First, to fulfill His Word to His own, who form His Church and bride, to receive them to Himself; and secondly, to fulfill God's promises to the Jews. His Church has a heavenly calling; Israel's calling is in contrast. His second coming will bring fulfillment to both expectations. It naturally follows that He will need to come for His own, first of all, and then with His own afterwards, to deliver Israel. The Word is explicit when it says, "He will come with ten thousands of His saints." If He is to come with them, then He must first come for them. This is why the apostle, by revelation, said: "The Lord Himself [shall] descend from heaven with a shout" (1 Thessalonians 4:16). This descent from Heaven is the first stage of His coming, and coincides with the first resurrection of believers in Christ. At the same time the living ones are changed, and together they meet the Lord in the air, to remain with Him forever.

During the period between these two stages of His coming, wonderful happenings take place in the Lord's presence, and dreadful times of wrath from God transpire on the earth.

The first stage therefore is His coming for the Church, to fulfill her heavenly calling; the second is for Israel's deliverance, to fulfill her earthly hopes.

The first stage is His coming into the air; the second is His coming to the earth.

The first stage is when He takes His own to be "forever with the Lord"; the second is when some are taken for judgment.

The first stage is the coming of the Lord Himself, the Saviour, the Lord Jesus Christ; the second is His coming as the Son of Man.

The first stage is when He will appear without sin unto salvation; the second is when He will come to take vengeance on His enemies.

The first stage is His coming in the twinkling of an eye (that is, secretly); the second is His coming openly and publicly, for every eye shall see Him.

The first stage is His appearing to His own as the Morning Star; the second is His arising on earth as the Sun of Righteousness.

The first stage was given by special revelation, not the subject of Old Testament prophecy; the second was foretold in the prophetic writings of the Old Testament.

The first stage will be foreshadowed by moral signs; the second will follow material signs.

The first stage is always looked forward to in the Word with joyful anticipation; the second is always spoken of with dread.

Individual believers, who together form the Church, will stand before the judgment seat of Christ immediately following the first stage of His coming, for John in his Epistle speaks of the possibility of some being "ashamed before Him at His coming." The implication is that it is a part of the same operation. The "bema" or judgment seat will be set up at once in the Lord's presence, and some Christians may very well be ashamed to see the poor results of their own life and work. The Greek word for judgment seat suggests a low dais or platform, literally "a step," where the umpire of the Greek games used to sit to give rewards and deck winners with laurel wreaths. It is never used in the New Testament in the sense of a judicial bench, so here in the presence of Christ there will be no judgment for condemnation. The simple but glorious fact is that the Lord Himself has borne all the condemnation which was due the sinner, now saved by grace.

Christ Jesus bore the sin and its judgment on the cross of Calvary, when by the Father, He was made sin for man (2 Corinthians 5:21), in the sense that man's sin was imputed to Him, so that His righteousness could be justly imputed to those who believe in Him. "There is therefore now no condemnation for those who are in Christ Jesus" (Romans 8:1). It will be a judgment of rewards for deeds done by the Christian when he was on earth. Wrongs perpetrated in this life will be seen by the Lord for what they are, and all will be righted then, with the suffering of loss for anything done in the power of the flesh instead of in reliance upon God, and anything attempted with motives for self-glory. "The fire shall try every man's work of what sort it is" (1 Corinthians 3:13 KJV). "No flesh shall glory in His presence" is the Lord's unalterable principle, which is operative now, and will be again in the New Jerusalem.

The rewards or "crowns" (see 1 Corinthians 9:25; 1 Thessalonians 2:19; 2 Timothy 4:8; James 1:12; 1 Peter 5:4) in that day are of five differing types: the incorruptible crown to those who subdue the corruptible, and keep under the body; the crown of rejoicing to the soul-winners; the crown of righteousness to second-coming lovers; the crown of life to those who suffer for His sake; finally, the crown of glory to steadfast elders. No elders will receive this crown for any of the deacons' practical work, for theirs is a spiritual ministry in the local church. This reward is solely for faithful under-shepherds in the church, for elders, pastors, and teachers.

This then will be the first placing and period of the New Jerusalem, after the rapture of the Church. This will be the Church's preparation for her presence at the marriage supper of the Lamb, and also for her manifestation over the earth during Christ's reign, which will follow.

The Marriage Supper in the New Jerusalem

It seems evident that it is just before the New Jerusalem comes down from God out of Heaven, that the marriage supper of the Lamb will be held there. It is after the supper that Heaven is opened, the Lord comes to earth to make war, and the armies of Heaven follow dressed in fine linen. At that time there will be the overthrow of the great whore, the unified system of world religions. In the marriage of the Lamb the Church takes the significant role of the bride, but the Lamb Himself receives all the glory, for it is His by right. It is not unexpected that the usual order is reversed: it is the marriage of the Bridegroom, rather than that of the bride. "The

Lamb is all the glory, in Emmanuel's land."

In preparation for the marriage of the Lamb, the bride makes herself ready by submitting to His authority at His judgment seat, and by dressing in fine linen, the symbol of her inward cleansing. Those guests at the wedding who are said to be blessed in their participation are Old Testament saints, and John the Baptist is included in "the friends of the bridegroom." A separate identity of Old Testament saints is obviously maintained in the New Jerusalem and in this connection we should observe that Abraham's hope was for a heavenly city rather than an earthly kingdom.

The Second Scene

The New Jerusalem comes out of Heaven, and she comes from God. This therefore implies that the saved have already inhabited the city in Heaven itself. This coming out of Heaven provides the second scene for the New Jerusalem, and it coincides with the coming of Christ in power and great glory to deliver His ancient people that remain after the great tribulation. It is this time of judgment and refining, of sifting and mourning, of repentance and final deliverance which is spoken of in great detail and in graphical terms both by Zechariah the prophet, and the Apostle John in the book of Revelation.

Details about the role of New Jerusalem during the millennium are stated in Revelation 21:9–22:5). This description is retrospective, following a brief word about the eternal state. There are several parts of the Scripture where the writer, by the Spirit, gives a brief introduction to a subject, and then refers back to it later on to give the details. There is no exception here, but only an

example of this procedure. Another example can be
seen in Revelation 14 with regard to Babylon.

The Apocalypse was never intended to make prophecies in chronological order. When John in this section
refers to nations of earth and kings, he can be speaking
only of the thousand-year period, for neither of them
are in the eternal state, which would not concern the
healing of the nations. New Jerusalem is destined to play
an important part in this age of sabbath rest. She will
bring light and guidance to the nations of the earth;
through her the light and glory of God will shine upon the
earth, and the tree of life not only bears fruit continuously for the pleasure of the inhabitants, but the leaves are for
the healing (or the health) of the nations. Indeed the
whole idea of the city descending out of Heaven to a place
over the earth is to bring light and blessing to the people
on the earth during the reign of our Lord. These Gentile
nations will be those who have survived the judgment of
the nations in the Day of the Lord, following Christ's
coming in power and glory. They will be the "sheep" as
opposed to the "goats" described by our Lord in the
Gospels. They will have acted favorably towards the Jewish nation called by our Lord, "My brethren," or perhaps
more importantly those who will have acted in a way acceptable to the 144,000 Jewish witnesses throughout the
earth during Daniel's seventieth week.

In many ways New Jerusalem is presented in prophecy as a contrast to the old Jerusalem on earth at this time.
The city on earth and the Jewish nation will enjoy peace
through the rule of our Lord on the throne of David, but
it will actually be through those in the New Jerusalem
above, who will be sharing His reign, that the light will
shine and the blessing will come. In the prophecy, "He

will sit on the throne of David," there is no suggestion that He will be there physically sitting for a thousand years on a throne in old Jerusalem. He will certainly come to the earth and to this Palestinian city and to the Mount of Olives, but His actual reign will be from the New Jerusalem above: "He shall reign over the earth." He will have absolute authority, and old Jerusalem will be His capital.

The Third Scene

At the time of the destruction of the earth and the first heaven, which follows the thousand years, the New Jerusalem it seems will be withdrawn, for we read of her returning to a position above the earth again, from God and out of Heaven the second time. The scene will then be cleansed and purified, ready for both Heaven and earth to become the dwelling place of God. A loud voice from His throne affirms, "Behold, the tabernacle of God is [with] men, and He shall dwell among them, and they shall be His people, and God Himself shall be among them" (Revelation 21:3).

This third scene for the New Jerusalem will be during the eternal state. This is the continuing city of which the writer of Hebrews speaks. The city will come from God, for "He hath prepared for them a city," and its place will be in the center of the new creation. God will make all things new, with the exception of the sea. "There [will be] no more sea." That which is symbolic of separation and turbulence, of restlessness and fear will be gone forever. Kings and kingdoms will have fallen for the last time, for this new universe will be theocentric and God shall be all in all.

It would be an impossibility to procure many details concerning New Jerusalem in this its third appearance, because prophecy deals only very briefly with the eternal state. It is occupied with this earth and its people, up to and including the thousand years. The blessed dead who die in the Lord, and those who are alive at His coming have been promised a resting place which is eternal, and the Bible speaks of only one such place: the little part of Heaven called New Jerusalem.

The Lower Heavens Will Burn Up

"The heavens will pass away with a roar and the elements will be destroyed with intense heat, and the earth and its works will be burned up" (2 Peter 3:10). But, " 'the new heavens and the new earth which I will make will endure before Me,' declares the LORD" (Isaiah 66:22). God promises at the end of the Revelation that He will make all things new, that is, all things of this universe. "I create new heavens and a new earth" (Isaiah 65:17), is a prophetic word truly expected, for the Saviour said, "Heaven and earth will pass away" (Matthew 5:18). This includes neither God's Heaven, nor God's people in Heaven, nor New Jerusalem, their heavenly abode. We read of "spiritual forces of wickedness in the heavenly places" (Ephesians 6:12), and earlier in the same book we are assured that the Lord Jesus has ascended far above all these heavens, to be in the dwelling place of God. These lower heavens, called the works of God's hands, shall perish, "But Thou dost endure" (Psalm 102:26).

Actually New Jerusalem never comes to earth. It is heavenly in origin and destiny. In the eternal state the city is never seen conforming to earthly forms. On earth the sun will still shine, there it will be the Son's radiance and His Glory shining forth. On earth there will be the usual day and night, but there the Lamb will be the light, and there will be no night.

The building of God which believers look forward to, according to Paul, is an eternal home in the heavens, not made with hands. This is the New Jerusalem, always in the heavens, sometimes over the earth, and sometimes in God's immediate Presence, but it is plain that the eternal home is heavenly, and that the heavenly home is eternal.

Jacob's dream will then be realized. He saw a ladder set up between heaven and earth. The two spheres are seen to be in intimate relationship. God's Presence will be known in both the new Heaven and the new earth. Ever since Pentecost God has always dwelt with His own, and the Lord Jesus, looking forward to this happy prospect said, "If anyone loves Me . . . My Father will love him, and We will come to him and make Our abode with him" (John 14:23). Paul later affirmed, "It is God who is at work in you, both to will and to work for His good pleasure" (Philippians 2:13).

New Jerusalem will be far beyond the influence of Satan in each of these three spheres. During the tribulation, when the Church is in Heaven at the judgment seat of Christ and at the marriage supper of the Lamb, Satan will be the leader of a trinity of evil upon earth, bringing confusion and war and final destruction, for God will use him finally to fulfill His own purpose of judgment for the Jews, and wrath to the godless nations. During the millennial reign of Christ, when the Church reigns with her Lord over the earth from the New Jerusalem, Satan will be bound until the end of the thousand years. It is

true he will then be released for a short while and will
deceive the nations once more, but the Church will be out
of his reach and influence at that time. His final attempt
to frustrate the divine plans will be thwarted when, at the
commencement of the eternal state, he is cast into the
lake of fire to suffer eternal torment. But New Jerusalem
will go on forever.

New Jerusalem Is Forever

The kingdom at the commencement of the eternal
state will be given up to the Father by the Son, and God
(I take that to mean the triune God) will be all in all in
both Heaven and earth. However, we see that New Jerusalem remains in the eternal state and she remains the
delight of the heavenly Bridegroom. Even then she is still
the bride, she is still new and fresh and bright, the people who form her are still the beloved of Christ, and this
rightful relationship will continue forever. Just as the
bride will continue forever in happiness and holiness, so
the unjust will be unjust still, and continue so forever.
There is no provision made even then for unjust persons
to be made just persons, or to make the unclean, pure.
The Saviour once said, "If you die in your sins, whither I
go you cannot come." The principle is that as one is
found when all has been made new, so one will remain
forever. No part will ever be found within this New Jerusalem for the wicked dead. All these who are to stand
before God at the judgment of the great white throne at
the end of the thousand years will receive just and righteous condemnation, for they are judged according to
their works.

15

NEW JERUSALEM, THE GOLD AND THE GLORY

Every believer in our Lord Jesus Christ is a citizen of the heavenly holy city, New Jerusalem. In anticipation of his future home the Christian is said to possess a "blessed hope" (Titus 2:13). This hope is an anchor to his soul, both sure and steadfast. Because of the certainty of reaching that happy home above he can sing!

Until then my heart will keep on singing,
Until then with joy I'll carry on;
Until the day my eyes behold the city,
Until the day God calls me home.
—Stuart Hamblen

Professor James Stewart speaks of different ways of seeing a city like London or Paris or New York: "Youth sees the city as the gateway to adventure, freedom, pleasure, and romance. The business man sees it as a place for carving out a successful career. The statistician sees it as a social unit, with so many parliamentary voters, so many housing estates and schools. The poet sees it as a fascinating silhouette against the sky. The moralist sees the city as a microcosm of humanity, with teeming thousands . . . men being born and dying and laughing and cursing." The city above will have new dimensions not known before. There will be pleasure for those within, for it is paradise. There will be joyful service, for its inhabitants will serve the Lord Christ and share His reign. The tree of life and the river of life will be there, in fulfillment of His promise to give to His own life more abundant. But above all their Lord will be there. They will see His face then, they will abide in His presence, they will worship at His feet. This holy communion and blessed intimacy will mean for them full identification with their Saviour and Lord.

> Face to face! O blissful moment!
> Face to face—to see and know;
> Face to face with my Redeemer,
> Jesus Christ who loves me so. . . .
> Face to face in all His glory,
> I shall see Him by and by!
> Mrs. Frank Breck

In His high-priestly prayer our Lord said: "Father, I desire that they also, whom Thou hast given Me, be with Me where I am, in order that they may behold My glory, which Thou hast given Me; for Thou didst love Me before the foundation of the world" (John 17:24). When the Christian dies he is absent from the body but present with the Lord, beholding His glory. "To day shalt thou be with Me in paradise" (Luke 23:43 KJV), said our Lord to the dying thief. At the coming of Christ for His Church the dead in Christ shall rise first, that is, the bodies in which they lived on earth will be raised and changed and fashioned like His body of glory. This will coincide with the living saints, caught up to meet the Lord in the air, when their bodies of mortality will be changed to immortality. "And so shall we ever be with the Lord" (1 Thessalonians 4:17). The body is not the man, it is only the house he lives in while on earth. The dead one in Christ, without his body, consciously enjoys the presence of Christ; but in his resurrection body he will recognize and enjoy the fellowship of others, too.

Although the Lord is very precious to believers, their present knowledge of Him is incomplete, because of sin; but then, not only will they know as they are known of God, but they will know Him perfectly. "My beloved is mine, and I am His" (Song of Solomon 2:16) will be the true relationship between Christians and Christ in that day. There will be no misery through boredom in His presence, for His "bond-servants shall serve Him" (Revelation 22:3). It will be their greatest joy to do His bidding and share not only His glory but His reign also.

The city, which is the bride of Christ, is significantly named "Jerusalem," the dwelling of peace. In this life Christians are brought into peace with God, who is the God of peace, and that is reconciliation. They also experience the peace of God keeping and guarding the heart and mind. But in the city of peace above, the experience will be perfect, in contrast to that of old Jerusalem, which should have been a city of peace and praise in the earth. Instead she became Sodom and Egypt, because she refused the Prince of Peace, who prophesied that peace would be hid from her eyes. The Church is the bride of Christ, the one He loves. He gave Himself for her that He might present her to Himself in stainless glory.

> He and I in that bright glory
> One deep joy shall share;
> Mine, to be forever with Him,
> His, that I am there.
>
> —Paul Gerhardt

The city is said to have the glory of God in it, and this shall shine in and through His own in that day. Glory is the outshining of one or more of the divine attributes. He "manifested forth His glory" when He turned the water into wine at the marriage feast in Cana of Galilee. He revealed His omnipotence and "His disciples believed in Him" (John 2:11). In the new home above there will be no hindrance to a full manifestation of His glory. Everything mentioned about the city by the Apostle John seems to show forth the glory of the Lord. The system of the illumination of the city is divine for God and the Lamb are the light, and the saved ones reflect that light. So do the streets, the walls, the foundations, and all that is in it—almost blinding with its dazzling brightness.

Saul of Tarsus on the way to Damascus saw light from Heaven greater and brighter than the noonday sun. Moses face shone with the light of God, and on the mount of transfiguration the light from the person and raiment of Christ in His glory was dazzling. No wonder Isaiah said (24:23), "The moon shall be confounded, and the sun ashamed" in that day. The city is celestial in origin, a product of almighty power and wisdom, and therefore of necessity the best that has ever been known, surely a reflection of God Himself.

Heavenly Gold

The materials of the New Jerusalem portray transcendent beauty, which can be rivaled by nothing on earth. It is most fitting as a habitation, first of all for God and His Son, and then for the people of God who form the bride of Christ. The city itself appeared to John as pure gold, bright as clear glass, shining with the glory of God.

Gold is often symbolic of glory, and John seems to alternate in his description between gold and glory, and glory and gold. He experiences something of the incommunicable mystical vision and, as far as words have power to tell, he describes the radiance of the Lamb and the glory of the Lord emanating freely on and from the faces of those who themselves form the holy city. Likewise the temple is God Himself and what light can compare with the light of His divine Presence? So John is attempting to convey by symbol and metaphor the brightness that struck him, as radiance from the Lamb dazzled his soul.

Psalm 45 has its historical basis in the marriage of Solomon to the daughter of the king of Egypt, but David here is referring to Christ and His bride. No doubt David was borne along by the Holy Spirit to speak of One who was greater than Solomon his son ("Behold a greater than Solomon is here"), and of another, the Church, who is greater than the daughter of the king of Egypt. Verse 6, "Thy throne, O God, is forever and ever," speaks of Christ, as is evident from Hebrews 1:8 where the writer uses this same verse to speak of our Lord. David by the the Spirit says of Him and of those in His Presence:

> My heart overflows with a good theme,
> I address my verses to the King;
> My tongue is the pen of a ready writer. . . .
> Kings' daughters are among Thy noble ladies;
> At Thy right hand stands the queen in gold from Ophir. . . .
> Then the King will desire your beauty;
> Because He is your Lord, bow down to Him.
> And the daughter of Tyre will come with a gift. . . .
> The King's daughter is all glorious within;
> Her clothing is interwoven with gold,

> She will be led to the King in embroidered work. . . .
> They will be led forth with gladness and rejoicing;
> They will enter into the King's palace.

The precious stones in the New Jerusalem reveal that the Lord will array His people with every variety of beauty, the beauty of the King Himself. It is an imputed righteousness. He bore their sin on the tree once, but then they will bear His holiness and comeliness in divine perfection, and it will shine like an array of precious stones. "So the beauty of the Church is set forth by a supernatural imagery, something quite beyond nature" (William Kelly). Perhaps jasper stone—"most precious . . . clear as crystal"—is meant to describe God's glory as far as it may be understood by one of His creatures, because no man can approach the glory of God. The New Jerusalem is the perfection of His glory, as He reveals Himself continually, with every facet of His divine attributes, to His own.

When the apostle was describing the city of jewels he may well have had in mind Isaiah 54:11-12: "O afflicted one, storm-tossed, and not comforted, Behold, I will set your stones in antimony, And your foundations I will lay in sapphires. Moreover, I will make your battlements of rubies, And your gates of crystal, And your entire wall of precious stones. . . . And the well-being of your sons will be great."

John saw the foundations of the walls garnished with precious stones. The first was jasper, though evidently not jasper as we know it, which is an opaque stone. The second is sapphire, blue and similar to a diamond in its hardness. The third is chalcedony, an agate from Chalcedon, also blue, but with colored stripes. The fourth is green, an emerald; the next is sardonyx, red with white stripes.

The sixth is red, the more common sardius stone. The seventh is crysolyte, pale green or golden and somewhat transparent. The eighth is the sea-green beryl; the ninth is topaz, which is more yellow and transparent too. The tenth, the chrysoprasus, is of a different shade of green. The eleventh is jacinth, violet in color, and the final foundation stone is amethyst, usually purple.

A closer look at the colors of these stones brings to mind the rainbow, and there may be some significance in that. In any case, the city itself and the walls and their foundations are described in these terms to portray the attributes of God shining forth in the beauty of holiness and the grace and blessing of those who are the objects of His salvation.

In the twelve foundations and twelve gates we see perfection portrayed, twelve being the number of administrative completeness or perfection in government. On the twelve foundations the names of the twelve apostles are written, bringing to mind the words of their Master: "You who have followed Me, in the regeneration when the Son of Man will sit on His glorious throne, you also shall sit upon twelve thrones, judging the twelve tribes of Israel" (Matthew 19:28). As in the Epistle to the Ephesians the Church is seen as a holy temple upon the foundation of the apostles and prophets, so this heavenly city here is founded on twelve chosen apostles, who in that coming sphere will be the representatives of the Church's rule and authority. The twelve gates are made of pearl in the vision, and so at every entrance there is a reminder of the one pearl of great price which the heavenly Merchantman bought with all He possessed. The most costly things of earth are thus used to reveal the dignified standing of those who enter the New Jerusalem.

Gates are for an entrance, but as these gates are never shut we conclude that they speak of liberty, too. They "shall go in and out, and find pasture" (John 10:9), said our Lord about His saved sheep. Not only the light but also the liberty of the children of God find perfection in this open city above. There are divine ministers at each of the twelve gates. The twelve angels are probably the welcoming committee rather than the protective or security guard, for God has decreed that nothing shall in any way enter into the city that defileth, or that worketh abomination. Only those with glorified bodies will ever be able to approach the city of God. The names of the twelve tribes are written on the gates of the city, for in the millennium the government of the earth is to be in the control of God's earthly people, restored to their own land and restored to favor among the nations, but under the jurisdiction of the Lamb and His bride in the New Jerusalem.

Happiness, Holiness, and Home

The happiness of the Church is seen in many ways. She has shared in Christ's rejection and now she shares in His glory and reign: "If we endure, we shall also reign with Him" (2 Timothy 2:12). Jonathan never shared David's reign because he let David, the anointed king, go out alone into the wilderness, while he returned to King Saul, his father, the man that God rejected because of his sin. When David returned to reign, Jonathan was dead. But not so Ittai the Gittite, who in later years followed David out of Jerusalem and across the brook Kidron into his rejection, for Absalom had stolen the throne. On the death of David's rebellious son, the king returned to reign and Ittai returned with him, to share the glory (see 2 Samuel 15:19-22).

We notice that in the New Jerusalem the Church will bear the image of the heavenly, and what a relief and comfort that will be after bearing, for so many years, the image of the earthly! Holiness means happiness too. The bride puts on her white garments. She has made herself ready for this occasion by accepting the preparation made for her through the death of Christ, His resurrection, and His imputed righteousness. She is a holy people, nothing that defileth has any association there, and the joy of the overcomer will be complete.

"And they sang a new song before the throne" (Revelation 14:3).

> I heard a thousand trumpets sounding out His glory
> Telling the story how He came on earth to die,
> I heard a million voices praise the name of Jesus,
> Singing in God's choir in the sky.

The angels can never sing the song of the redeemed, for "angels never knew the joy that our salvation brings," but their song of glory to the Lamb is a mighty chorus there on high.

In this scene the seal or sign that Christians are God's property is the possession of His Holy Spirit in their hearts and lives. The seal was always the evidence of ownership. Those on earth during the tribulation will need to have the seal or mark or number of the beast, the man of sin, on their foreheads before they can buy or sell. There will have to be the evidence that they belong to this man of perdition, and that they worship him. However, the name of God will be stamped on the foreheads of the saved in the New Jerusalem. This will be the mark of a permanent relationship with Him, while they abide with Him in their eternal home.

Home, Sweet Home, Forever

> Land of Emmanuel, Thou art home to me, because
>   My Lord is there
> It is a foreign land where He is not, however
>   sweet and fair!
> It is His presence in thee which causes thee to be
> No strange and foreign country, but home, true
>   home to me.

Revelation 22 commences with John getting a vision of the river of the water of life. The river is pure and free from pollution, because it flows not from earth, but from the throne of God. There is not a word to show that this river ever touches earth and those who dwell on it. It is divine in origin, flowing through a heavenly city for the refreshment of a glorified Church. "There is a river whose streams make glad the city of God, The holy dwelling places of the Most High" (Psalm 46:4).

There is no happiness where there is dust and drought, but this river brings life divine wherever it flows, and it is seen in contrast to the lake of fire, which is the second death. As this river proceeds from the throne of God, we are reminded of the Holy Spirit who proceeds from the Father, as our Lord said. "He who believes in Me, as the Scripture said, 'From his innermost being shall flow rivers of living water.' But this He spoke of the Spirit, whom those who believed in Him were to receive" (John 7:38). Those who drink on earth of that refreshing and

life-giving stream will drink anew and to the full throughout the unending day of glory.

Of special interest to all who have found themselves in their federal head, Adam, is the tree of life in
the New Jerusalem. One of the reasons why God drove
Adam and Eve from the garden following the fall, was to
prevent them from partaking of the tree of life, which
was not for them after they had sinned. In the eternal
home, however, the tree (or trees) of life will be there for
our use and the fruit will be sweet to our taste. During the
millennial age the leaves of this tree will be used for the
health of the nations. The fruit will not be for earth
dwellers, but the tree of life will bring some blessing from
God to men on earth in that day. The sin of man cut
him off from the tree of life, but the grace of God in
Christ brings him nigh once more, for "to him who over-
comes, I will grant to eat of the tree of life, which is in
the Paradise of God" (Revelation 2:7).

Arriving in New Jerusalem

Imagine one day stepping ashore, and finding it is
the golden shore, your eternal home. Imagine entering
through a huge pearl-like gate, the gate of glory. Imagine
walking along the shining streets of the city of God, the
New Jerusalem. Imagine clasping a loving hand in that
glad day, the once-pierced hand of your heavenly Bridegroom. Imagine your tears wiped away forever, and that
by the hand of the God of all comfort Himself.

> The glory shines before me,
> I cannot linger here!
> Though clouds may darken o'er me,

My Father's house is near. . . .
Beyond the storms I'm going,
Beyond this vale of tears,
Beyond the floods o'erflowing,
Beyond the changing years. . . .
The voice of Jesus calls me,
My race will soon be run
The glory shines before me:
The prize will soon be won.
                    —Hannah K. Burlingham

16

THE NEW JERUSALEM AND HER PURSUITS

While on this earth, waiting for the coming of the King, the Church is commissioned by her Head to occupy until He returns. She occupies herself in the first place with worship, for the Father seeks "the true worshipers [who would] worship the Father in spirit and truth" (John 4:23). She is a bond-servant also, called to serve the Lord Christ in fulfillment of His own great commission: "Go into all the world and preach the gospel to all creation" (Mark 16:15). She is not sent to convert the world, however, but to complete the Church (that is, by the enabling of the Holy Spirit), for God by His Spirit and through the Church is, in this present age, calling out from the world a people for Himself, to be the chosen bride for His Well-Beloved, His unique Son. She is occupied therefore in worship, in service, and of course in effective Christian living, as the Apostle Paul urges Christians to do: "Prove yourselves . . . children of God above reproach in the midst of a crooked and perverse generation, among whom you appear as lights in the world" (Philippians 2:15).

To some degree the pursuits of the Church in the New Jerusalem will be similar to her present occupation. At that time, in the actual presence of the Lord, to worship Him will be paramount: she will undoubtedly serve Him and share in the work of His reign, but rather than shine as a light herself, she will bask and "dwell forever in

His marvelous light" and then reflect that light to the nations on earth, for their blessing and guidance.

In 1 Thessalonians 4 the apostle describes the rapture of the Church: "We shall be caught up together with them" (our departed loved ones in Christ). "Wherefore comfort one another with these words." But he says something even more inspiring to the child of God: "We [shall] live together with Him. Wherefore comfort yourselves together" (1 Thessalonians 5:10-11 KJV). The bride's cherished hope and ambition is to be with her heavenly Bridegroom in His home above. It would be an impossibility for any believer to be in the presence of the gracious and glorified Son of God without sincerely worshiping Him. Our worship now is sometimes very weak and poor. It is even possible to misunderstand the idea completely, and deceive ourselves in believing that worship is going to church, perhaps, or listening to a sermon. To worship is to be led by the Spirit; to meditate on the glory of the Person of Christ; to know the enabling of the Spirit; to appreciate the value of the work of Christ; and to be moved by the same Holy Spirit to allow one's love to flow freely and unrestrained towards Christ Himself, who first loved us, and to God the Father, who gave His well-beloved Son to bear our judgment at Calvary. Love is the acid test of true worship.

No Man, Save Jesus Only

At that time, in the New Jerusalem, the Church will worship as she should without hindrances or distractions. Christ's glory will grip the vision and amazement, wonder, and adoration will be forthcoming immediately from His bride. John in his Gospel says, "We beheld His glory."

The Word of Life became not only visible in the incarnate Son of God, but audible and comprehensible and even tangible. We believe it was on the holy mount of transfiguration that John beheld His glory, when with the other favored disciples, Peter and James, he was encouraged to be occupied with Christ alone. Moses and Elijah were also there, and Peter, it seems, at first began to be interested in them. This however was disallowed by the Father, for a cloud obliterated the other two, and they saw no man save Jesus only. Then there followed the words of the Father, "This is My beloved Son . . . hear ye Him."

Both Moses and Elijah had remarkable experiences and they could have been excused if they had had the desire to discuss together each other's exodus, that is Moses' exodus from Egypt and Elijah's exodus from this scene. But no! their talk was about Christ and His exodus, which He was about to accomplish at Jerusalem. Just as King David was evidently delighted when his son Solomon was crowned king in Jerusalem, so here when Christ was transfigured into His kingdom glory His Father declared His pleasure in Him.

Just as on the mount of transfiguration (a foretaste of our Lord's coming glory), Old Testament saints and New Testament saints were all taken up with Christ, thus it will be in the New Jerusalem, His Person and His cross will be the theme of their song. The Old Testament saints had been looking forward to His cross work and the Church found salvation by looking back to it. Now, together in His presence, they worship Him and speak of His redemptive work with thankful hearts.

In the account of the transfiguration on the mount we find good evidence not only of life after death, but of the type of life after death for the saved, who will share His glory in the New Jerusalem. Moses and Elijah were alive as individuals and as continuing personalities. They were alive as human beings, and they are seen to be as conscious as ever they were. They were alive in glorified bodies to enjoy fellowship with one another. They were alive and in touch with the earthly scene. But above all else, they were alive to be taken up with Christ and His death at Calvary.

In the course of his minstry on prophetic subjects the writer is often asked such questions as: "What are we going to do in the New Jerusalem?" "Shall we be sad when we know the state of our unsaved friends?" "Shall we be able to pursue our own pastimes in which we now find so much pleasure?" The answer to all these questions must be that Christ and His glory will completely fill our gaze and satisfy our souls. We shall be so taken up with Him, His worship, His service, and His reign, that all other objects will fade, and it will be "Jesus only." As Asaph said when he found himself in the divine presence, "Whom have I in heaven but Thee? and there is none upon earth I desire beside Thee" (Psalm 73:25 KJV). One person recently wanted to be sure that there would be snow in the next life, because she loved to go skiing, whereas another wanted to bask in the sunshine forever. It is neither sun nor snow but only *the Son* who will satisfy the child of God in the New Jerusalem.

The Apostle John saw a multitude in our Lord's presence, saying with a loud voice, "Worthy is the Lamb that was slain to receive power and riches and wisdom and might and honor and glory and blessing [or thankfulness]" (Revelation 5:12). Now if He is the One to receive, then those before Him are the ones who will be giving, and the Church in the New Jerusalem will be doing that forever; giving unto Him, and that is worship. "Give unto the LORD glory and strength. Give unto the LORD the glory due unto His [holy] name. . . . O worship the LORD in the beauty of holiness" (Psalm 96:7 KJV).

The main reason for the new city coming out of God from Heaven, is that she might be over the earth during the millennium in the reign of Christ. Mankind was made by God and for God, as the Scripture affirms: "For [His] pleasure [we] were created" (Revelation 4:11 KJV). This purpose will then be realized to the full in the Church. To share in that reign will be her joyful and satisfying service and His good pleasure. "His bond-servants shall serve Him; and they shall see His face" (Revelation 22:3-4). "If we endure," the apostle wrote to troubled saints, "we shall also reign with Him" (2 Timothy 2:12).

Not that the Church will be on the earth, for although He "cometh with ten thousands of His saints" (Jude 14 KJV) the Bible nowhere teaches that she will remain on the earth during the reign of Christ, but she will be over the earth, reigning *in His reign.*

May we suggest this explanation: God now sees the Christian as being "in Christ," united to Him in a complete sense. The moment a sinner puts his trust in the Saviour, our Lord Jesus Christ, the Holy Spirit does a great work in joining him to His Lord in a full and eternal union. Henceforth God sees the Christian in His Son, accepted by God because he is in the Beloved One (see Ephesians 1:6 KJV). God reckons him to be in Christ's death also, because that which Christ did for him is reckoned by God as having been done by him. Therefore in God's sight he has died for his sin in another's death, that of his Saviour and Lord. "He who . . . died is freed [or justified] from sin" (Romans 6:7). So this then is the only judicial and righteous ground for the believer's justification. He is vindicated from his sin because he has died for it in the divine reckoning. God sees him in Christ's death, but more, God sees him in Christ's risen life, "You have died and your life is hidden with Christ in God" and "Christ . . . is our life." To make this real to His own in a practical way, God has given the Spirit of Jesus to indwell the heart and life of every Christian: "If anyone does not have the Spirit of Christ, he does not belong to Him" (Romans 8:9).

The sinner saved by grace is also joined by God to Christ in His present exaltation at God's right hand, at least God sees him in His Son's enthronement on high, "seated . . . with Him in the heavenly places" (Ephesians 2:6). Our Lord is in the place of authority in Heaven and the believer is in Him there also, according as God sees him, although in his own life he is still on earth. God has made believers in Christ one with their Lord in every way. In the New Jerusalem, therefore, the Church, still in Christ, in the divine recoming will be actually in Him in His reign over the earth, sharing His reign in that unique way and sharing His glory too.

So the Church will be in His presence and in His reign, exercising authority with Him over the place where He was once rejected, and where the Church also shared His rejection. The kings of the earth will bring honor and glory *unto* (*not* into) the Holy City to Jesus their King, and the Church will share in that honor. His victory will now be complete and she will share in the spoil. We may recall how King David, after his victory over the Amalekites, who had invaded and burned his city Ziklag and taken his loved ones and his men's wives captive, returned to the city and divided the spoil of his triumph, sending portions around the realm with his note: "Behold, a gift for you from the spoil of the enemies of the LORD" (1 Samuel 30:26). The Church will then share in the spoils of Christ's past victory, a victory actually gained at the cross, but then fully realized.

There will also be the diffusion of heavenly and divine principles and laws over the earth, for He will rule with a rod of iron and sin will not be allowed to rear its ugly head. It will be through the saints then with Him, that the Lord will thus claim that which is His by right and enter into His full inheritance. Part of the service in New Jerusalem will be the diffusion of light (a reflected light from the Lamb) by the Church to the nations of the earth. One aspect of the glory then revealed will be spiritual light, diffused by the Church to the nations. This will not become the natural light for the people of earth, but it will be light from Heaven to guide them into God's ways and God's truth. The sun will still shine in the heavens for the old Jerusalem and the nations on earth, but the *Son* will shine through the Church in the New Jerusalem to all the peoples who on earth shall dwell. Christians will reign therefore as kings and the nations will be the subjects in that day, as David said: "The whole earth [will] be filled with His glory" (Psalm 72:19). The exact kind of communications the New Jerusalem will have with the earth has not been specifically stated. We do know, however, that the Church will judge angels and the world (1 Corinthians 6:2-3), as well as reign with Christ.

The governing of the earth during the millennium will be through the nation of Israel, but Israel in turn will be governed from the New Jerusalem by the twelve apostles of the Lamb, and by the Church, Christ Himself being over all, God's King. That is the time of the fulfillment of the prophecy that He will see of the anguish of His soul and be satisfied (see Isaiah 53:11). By that time also the nations of the earth will be bringing their glory and honor to Him. Those that remain of Israel will have been saved and cleansed. For them there will be untold blessings in His reign over the earth and the redeemed will be as His bride in His presence, to go no more out forever.

Fellowship Without Fault

Christian fellowship in this life is one of God's best blessings. In every far-flung field of the world the Lord has His own, and fellowship over the Word, in united prayer, and around a meal table is an experience never to be forgotten by those who have enjoyed it. Sometimes, however, the fellowship is marred by criticism; although God remembers we are but dust and failing humans, others are inclined to forget this. All God's people are looking forward with joyful anticipation to the delight of fellowship with each other when all have been made perfect.

> To dwell above with saints we love
> Indeed that will be glory,
> But to dwell below with saints we know,
> That is another story!

God will see to it then that there will be fellowship without fault, communion without conflict, and devotion without disagreement. The gatherings around the throne of God in the New Jerusalem will be with openness and fullness of grace with "a wonderful spirit-to-spirit communion of radiant personalities," as DeHaan describes it.

17

THE NEW JERUSALEM AND HER MISSING THINGS

Some of the most significant things about the New Jerusalem will be the things that are absent from it. There will be no temple in the New Jerusalem although, according to the Prophet Ezekiel, there will be a temple in the old Jerusalem on earth. This will be one of the greatest contrasts between the two. There will be no need in the New Jerusalem of a special mode of access to God, as there will be on earth, for there the access to Him will be immediate. God's Presence was concealed in the Temple of old, for the veil hung between His people and the most holy place, but there will be no veil, no concealment, and no barriers in that city on high. The Temple of old was a sign in itself of the presence of sin, for in it God was hidden and man was kept at bay. In the New Jerusalem there will be nearness, and no need of the Temple, for they shall see His face. He Himself therefore will be the Temple. "The Lord God, the Almighty, and the Lamb are its temple" (Revelation 21:22).

So the place where "the pure in heart . . . shall see God" will be the New Jerusalem. Moses served God for eighty years and it was one of his greatest desires to see God face to face. "Show me Thy glory," he asked God, but in answer God plainly said, "You cannot" (Exodus 33:18,20). However, when mankind will be redeemed and perfected, God will reveal Himself to His own, when they are dwelling in their glorified bodies. There will be no sun, no created light, no candle, no artificial light in that abode. No earthly lights, nor even lights from the heavenly skies will be needed there; "the city [had] no need of the sun" (Revelation 21:23). Terrestrial light fades for those who "dwell [forever] in His marvelous light." "The glory of God [lighted] it," so the outshining of all the attributes of Deity will lighten that great city, and the Lamb will cause the light to shine within and around His own. Not only so, but the light will be diffused by the city dwellers to the people of earth, bringing spiritual and heavenly blessings to them, during His reign over them.

Once the world knew not His own, because it knew Him not; but then the world will know them, and the blessing they bring through the reflected light of God. It is admitted that God's people today sometimes fail in their calling to "appear as lights in the world" (Philippians 2:15), but then they will diffuse divine light in such a way that earth dwellers will receive it and see and know.

No Separation Nor Sin

The scriptural symbol for separation will be gone. "There is no longer any sea" (Revelation 21:1), meaning the sea and the oceans as we know them. No dangers from the deep, no perils in the waters may also suggest that there will be no divisions among the saved in that day of true ecumenicalism.

No sin of any kind, nor the defilement it brings will enter those pearly gates, for "grace [will] reign through righteousness to eternal life" (Romans 5:21). No corruption brought about by the fall of man, and no deceit brought about by the father of lies will delude any in that abode. That wretched thing which destroys lives, wrecks homes, and fills institutions now, will be absent then, O glorious day.

No curse will be known in the city of gold. The consequences of sin will never again bring men to despair, for their Saviour is with them. He bore the curse on the tree to redeem them from the curse of a broken law (see Galatians 3:13), and to save them from the curse imposed at the fall: "Cursed is the ground because of you" (Genesis 3:17). Today the farmer sows his seed, and behold a harvest of weeds! He then attempts to cure the crop's diseases and eliminate the weeds with modern chemicals, but in so doing he often creates many damaging side effects to those who might eat his produce, and also to birds and insects which would otherwise act as a natural pest control. So a vicious circle of disease and ruin develops; but not so in that land on high. One of the sweetest notes struck in the whole of the Bible is this: "There shall no longer be any curse" (Revelation 22:3).

"There shall be no night there" (Revelation 21:25). No nights of loneliness or despair, no long night vigils, waiting for the morning light, no nights of suffering or sorrow, no nights of weakness and fatigue. It will be one long and glorious untiring day, "neither day nor night; but it will come about that at evening time there will be light" (Zechariah 14:7). See the contrast here between this wonderful day in glory and the day and night on earth, and even of that in the lake of fire where the devil and the beast and the false prophet will be tormented day and night forever (see Revelation 20:10).

"Its gates shall never be closed" (Revelation 21:25). It was usual for gates of cities in the east to be closed at night, but as there is no night there, the Word is really saying that the gates are never closed at all. There will be no dread of enemies breaking in. The affirmation, "Its gates shall never be closed," is evidence that there will be no danger. The angels at the gates are the guardians and the walls are very high, speaking of eternal security. Today in our larger cities, one is afraid to go out at night, even during the day in some places. Those driving in broad daylight feel a need to lock their auto doors. Parents hesitate to allow their children to go unaccompanied down the road to the playground or to the store. In the New Jerusalem they will know no fear, for there is no armed robbery, no mugging, rape, or drug addiction.

No stranger ever enters the holy city, only those who can feel at home with the Lord. These are at peace in His presence, their faith rooted in Him and His righteousness imputed to them. Only those whose names are written in the Lamb's book of life are there. "A book of remembrance was written before Him for those who fear the LORD and who esteem His name" (Malachi 3:16).

In Thy book where glory bright
Shines with never fading light,
Where Thy saved Thou dost record;
Write my name, my name, O Lord!

In the New Jerusalem there is no more ignorance, for then shall we "know fully, just as [we] have been fully known" (1 Corinthians 13:12). Earthly knowledge will vanish away, as well as earthly ignorance. Knowledge is sometimes a scarce commodity on earth, for true knowledge is of God, and "The fear of the LORD is the beginning of knowledge" (Proverbs 1:7). But when His own find themselves in the presence of the Omniscient God in their glorified bodies, with minds so clear and perfected intelligences, how different it will be!

Peace and no more war is the blessed hope of the child of God. "What is the source of quarrels and conflicts among you?" asked the Apostle James (4:1-2). "Is not the source your pleasures that wage war in your members? You lust and do not have; so you commit murder. . . . So you fight." Desire will be completely satisfied for those in the holy city, and war will be a thing of the past. The Prince of Peace will reign supreme in the millennial age and that is only the vestibule of the eternal state of peace and joy.

No works of earth will be seen. Men's construction and scientific achievements will not be used. No skyscrapers or deep tunnels, no air or ocean liners, no medical science, computers, or robots will be needed there. No remolding of earth's atoms occurs, for the Scripture is definite when it says these things will "pass away . . . be burned up . . . dissolved" (2 Peter 3:10-11 KJV).

The old enemy, time, will be no more. Here we are always struggling against time, but there, no tight schedules will concern God's redeemed. Although during the one thousand years, the end of that period of time will be awaited on earth, in the eternal state of the New Jerusalem, time will not exist. No days, no nights, no clocks or even sand glasses, just one long beautiful eternal day.

The first tragic result of the fall of man will be eradicated for those of the heavenly city, for "there shall no longer be any death" (Revelation 21:4). Each one will already be in possession of God's gift in Christ, eternal life. All will have access to the tree of life and also the river of life, which flows freely for all. Everything speaks of life in an abundant sense. The last enemy, death, will be then "swallowed up in victory" (1 Corinthians 15:54). To every home on earth, and even to the happiest abodes, death comes and comes again, but in that home in the heavens never a victim will it find. For all men here death is a necessity, with only one exception, and that is Christ Himself. For Him death was an obedience: "He . . . became obedient unto death" (Philippians 2:8 KJV). He willingly died in obedience to the Father's will so that men might live through His atoning death.

> He Satan's power laid low,
> Made sin, He sin o'erthrew;
> Bowed to the grave, destroyed it so
> And death by dying slew.
>
> —W. Gandy

That is the precise reason why death is no more in the New Jerusalem. No hopeless deathbed vigils in the new city, no funerals will traverse the streets. The reign of sin unto death for its inhabitants will be over forever.

Starvation will never be known in that day. His fruit will be sweet to the taste, and the variety should be also noted, "twelve manner of fruits" (Revelation 22:2). The continuity of the supply of the tree of life is assured: "the tree . . . yielded her fruit every month." In this world there is never enough for everyone; millions starve each year through failure of crops, distribution, or funds. But then God will supply, through His riches there in glory, all that is needed. Even the leaves of the trees will be used to good effect, for they shall be for the health of the nations.

There is no pain in the Jerusalem above (Revelation 21:4). The sign of suffering and testing is over. Disease, accidents, and injuries through warfare bring pain and suffering to untold millions in this poor earth. How thankful are those who find temporary relief through physicians, and medicine of one kind or another. But think of meeting the Great Physician in the place He has gone to prepare, and of using the "balm in Gilead," not for some moments of relief from pain, but as an eternal cure.

God will see to it that there are no tears in His home. Even the symbol for sorrow will be gone forever, "He shall wipe away every tear from their eyes" (Revelation 21:4). It is not Gabriel who does it, although he stands in the presence of God, ready to do His bidding. No command is given to anyone to wipe away the tears from the eyes of one-time earth dwellers; God does it Himself. Tears are commonplace in this scene because of the tragedy, heartache, and remorse within "this place of tears." Anguish of soul, memory of the big mistake will often move men and women to weep. But God has promised in His Word to change sorrow and sobbing into a spirit of praise, and to give for misery and mourning the oil of joy. No tears of misfortune or bereavement, no tears of persecuted innocence, no tears of contrition, penitence, or disappointment will ever be seen in the New Jerusalem. The fearful are excluded (Revelation 21:8), those who through the fear of men refuse to receive Jesus Christ as their own personal Lord and Saviour.

No unbelievers will ever walk the streets of the New Jerusalem (1 John 5:4). Overcomers, not unbelievers, inhabit that place. It is true that at this present time we may overcome and enjoy the blessedness of overcomers by exercising faith in God. "This is the victory that has overcome . . . even our faith." But everyone we shall meet in the concourses of the celestial city will be an overcomer! No sodomites or those guilty of unnatural lustful crimes against mankind will have a place in the order of God's tomorrow. These are called "abominable" ones for they defile themselves with their own abominations. "God gave them over in the lusts of their hearts to impurity, that their bodies might be dishonored among them" (Romans 1:24), a solemn warning indeed to people of this generation too. The apostle says, "No immoral or impure person . . . has an inheritance in the kingdom of Christ and God" (Ephesians 5:5). No sex perverts will be there. No murderers are seen in the Jerusalem above, for it is treason for anyone to deface his Maker's image.

God in His righteousness cannot clear the guilty (unless the guilty one believes in Jesus), and for this cause "the wrath of God comes upon the sons of disobedience" (Ephesians 5:6). No fornicators or whoremongers will be there. That God will judge them is directly stated (Hebrews 13:4), and they certainly would never be found in a holy place, looking into the face of a holy God and worshiping a holy Saviour. No sorcerers or those who commerce with evil spirits can enter God's holy city (Revelation 21:8), for this is not only a lust of the flesh, as Paul puts it, but it is a working of Satan and has no part in Heaven. Moses declared that for such the punishment would be the death of the body, but in the book of Revelation it is their final doom which is pronounced.

No idolaters will find their way into the presence of the Living God, for our God is a jealous God who in the beginning said, "You shall have no other gods before Me" (Exodus 20:3). Worshipers of dead images have had very little success in this life, for their gods "have ears, but they cannot hear," and their gods "have eyes, but they cannot see," and their gods "have feet, but they cannot walk," and "those who make them will become like them" (Psalm 115:6-8). Therefore, any attempt of idolaters to gain entrance there must be in vain, for they have never learned to "worship in the Spirit . . . and put no confidence in the flesh" (Philippians 3:3).

No false witnesses or liars will have a portion in the realm of God's tomorrow. They are of their father the devil, for he was a liar from the beginning, and they are followers of antichrist who denies the Father and the Son (1 John 2:22). In a place where the Father and the Son form the Temple and reveal their glory to their own, no one who belongs to Satan, who follows his emissaries or practices his deceptions, can ever hope to find a home.

Positively, Only Glory

With so many of these things missing and with all evil persons eliminated it must be only glory by and by for the redeemed in the New Jerusalem. As this is still the day of grace, however, and the day of salvation too, none will be denied a place in the mansions above who show "repentance toward God and faith in our Lord Jesus Christ" (Acts 20:21).

> The New Jerusalem on high has charms beyond our ken,
> When there, its glories we'll confess,
>   Surpass the praise of men.
> O glorious city of our God, O pure and pleasant place,
> In thee no sin, no curse is found,
>   Of sorrow not a trace.

18

THE TWO JERUSALEMS IN THE ETERNAL STATE

The glimpses we have of the eternal state in the Scriptures are very rare and indeed lacking in detail, but sufficient is stated to assure the Christian of the eternal glory which awaits him. The prophetic Scriptures are given to man to show God's purposes for His creatures in time, for Jews, Gentiles, and the Church of God; but none of these distinctions will be known in eternity. It is amazing that the God of eternity has such interest in the sons of time and that He has shown such matchless grace to His erring creatures. "The eternal God is [your] refuge, and underneath are the everlasting arms" (Deuteronomy 33:27). The subject of prophecy is not the unfolding of God's final blessing in eternity for those participating in the new Heaven and the new earth, although naturally this is mentioned in connection with the one great purpose of God to vindicate His Son on the earth and in time.

It is revealed that there will be a new Heaven and new earth in the eternal state. It is shown that the New Jerusalem will exist as in the millennium and it will continue to be the actual company of the saints in Heaven. In the new earth there will be no sea, which I believe should be taken literally, but there is nothing to suggest that there will be no Palestine or no Jerusalem. In fact Isaiah assures us that Jerusalem will enjoy the blessing of God continuously through the eternal state, as we shall see later.

The covenants God made with Israel guarantee the land of Palestine as theirs forever with earthly and spiritual blessings for His chosen people in perpetuity.

Events in Their Order

The order of events leading up to the eternal state demands a brief resume. During the millennial reign of Christ the earth will be full of the knowledge of the Lord as the waters cover the sea (see Isaiah 11:9). Man will be made to learn of God and His righteousness by imputation through a work of grace in the individual heart. Following the release of Satan, it will be seen that many of the unregenerate on earth will yield to his temptations to rebel at the rule of God's King in Jerusalem, nevertheless "He must reign until He has put all His enemies under His feet" (1 Corinthians 15:25). Although this will be Satan's last stand, with the use of all his powers, the power of Christ and the fire sent from Heaven will utterly consume these adversaries, and this will be the final judgment of God on the earth itself.

Next in order will be the casting of the devil into the lake of fire. He will have made his last vain stand against the Lord and His Christ, and then he will meet his eternal doom. There is not only to be a new Heaven for eternity, and a new earth for eternity, but the suffering and separation in the place prepared for the devil and his angels will be eternal too. (See Revelation 19:20, cf. Revelation 20:10.)

The great white throne of judgment will then be set up in the presence of God, and the wicked dead will be raised to stand before it in the presence of God's Son. The Apostle Paul, addressing the men of Athens in the court of Areopagas, said that God has not only made an appointment for all to be judged, but He has appointed a day for the judgment, a place for the judgment, and also the Judge, the Man whom He has ordained. "He has fixed a day in which He will judge the world in righteousness through a man whom He has appointed, having furnished proof to all men by raising Him from the dead" (Acts 17:31). The Scripture does not speak of any righteous dying during the millennium, so the resurrection, following Satan's last struggle, is only for the wicked dead.

The Triune God to Reign Forever

The first resurrection will have been completed before the millennial reign commences. The kingdom reign of Christ on earth will be given up to God the Father at the end of the thousand years, and as the saved enter into their experience of the eternal state, God Himself, that is the triune God—Father, Son, and Holy Spirit—will be all in all. It cannot mean that Christ will cease to reign, but the special reign over the earth of the Man Christ Jesus will give place to the eternal reign of God and of His Christ by the Divine Spirit. Neither the vindication of Christ, nor His personal glory, will in any way be affected by this surrender to the Godhead in its complete fullness. God as God will take the place of absolute supremacy through all eternity. The human kingdom of Christ will end after a thousand years, but not so the divine kingdom over all Heaven and earth; it is eternal. "Then comes the end, when He delivers up the Kingdom to the God and Father, when He has abolished all rule and all authority and power. . . . The last enemy that will be abolished is death" (1 Corinthians 15:24,26).

The enemy Gog and Magog will be the first to be abolished at the end of His reign. These are men filled with bitterness and gross ingratitude for the blessing brought by Christ in His reign. They will have shown no response to Christ, but will show eager response to Satan's revengeful strategy. The evil influence of Satan will be abolished when the deceiver himself is cast into the lake of fire, ending his deceptive cunning through the centuries. Death is the last enemy to be abolished, for when sin is judged and Satan is cast to his doom and even the heaven and earth are burned up, death cannot come where sin shall never be known, in the new Heaven and the new earth wherein dwells righteousness.

A Complete Re-Creation

The first heaven, the atmospheric heavens, will be burned up, as will the earth before the eternal state actually commences. When God says He will shake heaven and earth, we presume this is to be part of the same process of complete finality and re-creation for both. It may well be that the second Heaven also will be included in the burning, for that too (the heaven of space) has been polluted by Satan and to some small degree by sinful man. "The heavens will pass away with a roar and the elements will be destroyed with intense heat, and the earth and its works will be burned up" (2 Peter 3:10-13).

The third Heaven which is the dwelling place of God and the home of the saved will never need a re-creation. This is the place to which our Lord ascended, far above all heavens. Time will be no more when the earth and all that is therein will be burned up by the flames of divine retribution. Eternity cannot really be said to begin after that, for there is no beginning of eternity, just as there is no ending; but eternity will begin for the creatures of time with the making of the new Heaven and new earth which they will inhabit. "It is done," said the One who sat upon the throne. These same words were used in Revelation 16–17 at the completion of the outpouring of wrath; now it is said at the completion of the re-creation.

Done is the work that saves . . . for the Saviour on the cross cried, "Finished." Done is the work of justice . . . as in Revelation, God in His justice will pour out the judgments. Done is the work of re-creation . . . and the One who will do it is the Alpha and Omega, the beginning and the ending, and all in between is inferred also, God over all and God in all, blessed forever.

From Isaiah's prophecy we gather that Jerusalem in the Holy Land will again be in existence in the new earth, although this is often quoted as referring to the thousand-year period. The context, however, makes it quite plain that the eternal state is meant: "Behold, I create new heavens and a new earth; And the former things shall not be remembered or come to mind. . . . For behold, I create Jerusalem for rejoicing, And her people for gladness. I will also rejoice in Jerusalem, and be glad in My people; And there will no longer be heard in her the voice of weeping and the sound of crying" (Isaiah 65:17-19). "Then they shall bring all your brethren from all the nations . . . to the LORD. . . . to My holy mountain Jerusalem. . . . For just as the new heavens and the new earth which I make will endure before Me, declares the LORD, so your offspring and your name will endure" (Isaiah 66:20-22).

The New Jerusalem in the new Heaven is undoubtedly eternal. William Kelly says: "Although John seems to go back to the New Jerusalem in the millennium its intrinsic blessedness and glory will abide forever." Saved Israel will be on earth in Jerusalem and Palestine generally during the eternal state, just as the Church will be in Heaven in the New Jerusalem in the order of God's tomorrow.

Similar words are used by the prophet concerning old Jerusalem: "The city of the LORD, the Zion of the Holy One of Israel. . . . I will make you an everlasting pride. . . . Your people . . . will possess the land forever" (Isaiah 60:14-15,21). In Daniel's vision the word given to him was: "Seal up the prophecy for the time is not yet," but here in Revelation 22 the time has come for John to receive a short glimpse of God's future program. The proper season (for so the original word means) has then arrived for the unveiling of things yet to come to pass.

So there is to be a new Heaven and a new earth, for God said: "Behold, I am making all things new" (Revelation 21:5). This new creation will not be some temporary covering to hide the past tragedies of the centuries, but the earth will be remade by a definite act of creation and as the scene for the eternal theocratic kingdom of God. It will be the dwelling place of those who come through the millennial reign on earth, and the new Heaven (and the New Jerusalem will come down from God to be part of this) is for the raised and changed saints, still in their glorified bodies. The Church with the Old Testament saints will enjoy forever the new Heaven. The Jews and Gentile nations from the millennium will inhabit the new earth, although in the eternal state there will not be national distinctions as such, for the people of earth will be known simply as "men."

The Everlasting Ages

In stating the contrasts between the position, as it was shown in the book of Genesis, and that as we see it in the book of Revelation, the final and complete fulfillment of God's eternal purposes will be seen.

In the original state the earth was first created, in the eternal state the earth will be re-created.

In the original state man's home was an earthly garden; in the eternal state, the home of the saved will be a heavenly city.

In the original state, the first Adam brought in the fall; in the eternal state the Second Adam will bring in the glory.

In the original state Satan commenced his great deception for all times; in the eternal state God ends the activities of Satan for all eternity.

In the original state, man's sin brought separation from his God; in the eternal state, Christ's redemption will bring to him the continual presence of God.

Mankind will be in everlasting conscious existence, while God will be in everlasting control, the new Heaven and new earth will be in everlasting renewal, and Satan will be in everlasting punishment. The unending ages of the ages is the meaning of everlasting, and this eternity is the same eternity (there are not two eternities) as was before the creation of man, the only difference being: through the matchless grace of God, we will be there!

BIBLIOGRAPHY

Alderman, Paul R. Jr. *The Unfolding of the Ages.* Neptune, New Jersey: Loizeaux Brothers, 1954.

Anderson, Sir Robert. *The Coming Prince.* Grand Rapids, Michigan: Kregel.

Beck, M.A. *A Short History of Israel.* London: Hodder and Stoughton.

Bruce, F.F. *The Dawn of Christianity.* Exeter: Paternoster Press.

Chafer, Lewis Sperry. *Systematic Theology.* Grand Rapids, Michigan: Zondervan.

Darby, J.N. *Notes on the Apocalypse.*

DeHaan, R.W. *Our Heavenly Home.* (booklet) Grand Rapids, Michigan: Radio Bible Class.

————, *The Valley of Dry Bones.* (booklet) Grand Rapids, Michigan: Radio Bible Class.

English, E. Schuyler. *Re-Thinking the Rapture.* Neptune, New Jersey: Loizeaux Brothers, 1954.

Freel, William. *Survival?* London: The Berrico Group of Companies.

Gaebelein, Arno C. His various studies in prophecy.

Grant, F.W. *The Revelation of Jesus Christ.*

Ironside, H.A. *Lectures on the Revelation.* Neptune, New Jersey: Loizeaux Brothers, 1920.

————, Notes on Zechariah, in *Notes on the Minor Prophets.* Neptune, New Jersey: Loizeaux Brothers, 1909.

Jennings, F.C. *Studies in Revelation.*

Jewish National Fund. *A Nation Reborn.* London: Jewish National Fund.

————. *A Time-Chart of Jewish History.* London: Jewish National Fund.

Lambert, Lance. *Israel, A Secret Documentary.* Wheaton, Illinois: Tyndale.

Lang, G.H. *The Revelation of Jesus Christ.* London: Oliphants, 1945.

MacArthur, Jack. *Revelation, an Exposition.* Wheaton, Illinois: Tyndale.

Newell, William R. *Book of The Revelation.* Chicago, Illinois: Moody.

Olson, Arnold. *Inside Jerusalem, City of Destiny.* Glendale, California: Regal, G/L.

Ottman, Ford C. *Unfolding of the Ages in the Revelation.* Grand Rapids, Michigan: Kregel.

Pache, R. *The Founding of the Kingdom.*

Pentecost, J. Dwight. *Things to Come.* Grand Rapids, Michigan: Zondervan.

Ryrie, Charles Caldwell. *Dispensationalism Today.* Chicago, Illinois: Moody.

Scott, Walter. *Exposition of the Revelation of Jesus Christ.* London: Pickering and Inglis.

Seiss, Joseph. *The Apocalypse.* Grand Rapids, Michigan: Zondervan.

Showers, Renald E. *What on Earth Is God Doing? Satan's Conflict with God.* Neptune, New Jersey: Loizeaux Brothers, 1973.

Smith, Wilbur M. *The Israeli-Arab Conflict and the Bible.* Glendale, California: Regal, G/L.

Tatford, F.A. *Daniel's Seventy Weeks.* (article)
——— , *Prophecy's Last Word.* London: Pickering and Inglis.

Van Gorder, Paul R. *The Meeting in the Air.* (booklet) Grand Rapids, Michigan: Radio Bible Class.

Walvoord, John F. *Armageddon, Oil, and the Middle East.* Grand Rapids, Michigan: Zondervan.

——— , *Armageddon, Oil, and the Middle East Crisis.* Grand Rapids, Michigan: Zondervan.

——— , *The Millennial Kingdom.* Grand Rapids, Michigan: Zondervan.